WHOSE EARTH?

CHRIS SEATON

CROSSWAY BOOKS

First edition 1992

ISBN 1 85684 033 6

Typeset by Avocet Typesetters, Bicester, Oxon
Printed in Great Britain for Crossway Books, Kingfisher House, 7 High Green, Great Shelford, Cambridge by Cox & Wyman Ltd, Cardiff Road, Reading

DEDICATION

To Sam and to Poppy. That they might become friends of God and true friends of his earth.

CONTENTS

ACKNOWLEDGEMENTS

The writer of Proverbs tells us that "the way of a fool seems right to him, but a wise man listens to advice." Without the wisdom, love and advice of a number of friends this book would not be what it is.

I am particularly grateful to Jon Baker, Andrea Clarke, Barbara and Paul Coaker, Roger Ellis, Dave Evans, Martin Goldsmith, Roger Mitchell and Martin Scott – all very busy people who gave some of their valuable time to read parts of the manuscript. They helped me to iron out some quirks in my writing style, my science and my theology. Some of them did not find rest after reading my manuscript but were pestered by me with further letters and phone calls – they were all very constructive.

In an effort to help me keep up to date with developments in the fast-changing scene of environmentalism, a number of people plied me with articles, papers and sundry cuttings. Amongst these Mike Morris and his staff at the Evangelical Alliance, few of whom I have yet met, were prolific. Alison Beadsworth and Rachel Bentley at the Body Shop together with Dave Evans and Rachel Searle also helped considerably.

Without my own computer I have been dependant upon the flexibility and generosity of friends who could assist in this department. Bob Lock and his wonderful family deserve special mention here, supplying not only undisturbed use of computer, but also hot drinks, chocolates and the occasional chilli con carne! However Nikki Gilbert, Murray Jacobs and the Revelation office staff also helped. Indeed

Sarah Wilcock and the whole posse at our chaotic office were of enormous help in many ways and deserve my thanks.

When the unthinkable happened and I lost four chapters on both my work disk and on the back-ups, it was Sarah Gledhill and Janet Lock who kindly typed them back for me. Thanks – you saved my life!

I have received a great deal of encouragement and support from so many friends in Revelation Church, and from those in other Pioneer churches. I am as grateful to those who have disagreed with me on some points, and who have taken the trouble to say so, as I am to those who share my views. Debate has exposed some of my errors and sharpened my own ideas. Among the former category, Pete Gilbert, Kevin Allan and one or two TIE Teamers particularly come to mind. Above all, the leadership, love and vision of Gerald Coates, and the friendship and example of Roger Ellis have done so much to shape me, and therefore the content of this book.

The people at Crossway books have been a tremendous help. Christopher Catherwood's expertise and enthusiasm for the project have made me feel secure in my writing. The mysterious reader known to me as "Dr. X" has played a significant part in shaping up the book.

I owe a great debt to my parents who brought me up to believe in God and to love the countryside. Being told not to chuck your sweet wrappers out of the car window lays an important foundation in a young life. Green living must always begin at home.

In writing this book I have gained a fresh sense of wonder at the world that God has given us. The Psalms have come alive to me and I have sensed God's exquisite presence and involvement in my task on many occasions. The work of the musician Ian White, who has set many psalms to music, has been an invaluable inspiration.

Of the many other people who have helped me in different ways, there are two more whom I wish to acknowledge and thank especially. One is Mike Morris, a dear friend and colleague who suggested I write this book in the first place.

He has fought for me, listened to me and believed in me when I needed it most. The other person is my long-suffering wife, Charlotte. She has made many sacrifices to enable me to keep on working. It is no sentimental exaggeration to say that without her love and support, this book would not have been written. Thank you both, so much.

Finally, the usual exclusion clause: everything you like in this book can be attributed to my brilliance; anything you don't like is bound to be the fault of someone named above (or should that be the other way round?!)

FOREWORD

Chris Seaton: a name to conjure with. Young, radical and an ornithologist. Husband, father and a friend. Church planter, politician and now a writer. All this achieved by age 30: a remarkable accomplishment.

A lawyer by training Chris turned from practising law to plant a church. A handful of people soon grew to the place where they could themselves plant a congregation.

Always passionate in his beliefs Chris took up the whole green agenda and decided to write. I had a hand in persuading Chris to write and believe it has proved one of my better suggestions.

Motivation and challenge are part and parcel of Chris' character. This combined with an intelligent, thoughtful approach guarantees a refreshing competence in an age of superficiality. No disengaged overview here: rather an informed insight with radical proposals for action. Chris always demands action!

A shared love of cricket has further endeared this dynamo to me. After all can anyone who enjoys the sounds of summer, leather on willow, be anything other than a highly reputable fellow.

With the ability to relate to all ages and backgrounds (I've yet to meet someone who has not enjoyed half an hour of Chris' company) one can with certainty recommend this fine tome knowing that whether you are informed on the subject or ignorant, with highly developed opinions or with none, with aspirations towards academic excellence or without you will be entranced, informed and enabled by the following pages.

Once you have read it remember to recommend it to your friends.

Mike Morris
International Secretary of the Evangelical Alliance

INTRODUCTION

The market is not poorly supplied with varieties of the Christian paperback. If your bookshelf is anything like mine, it contains many a volume bought in an enthusiastic moment, or received as a well-meant gift. Many of these have one thing in common – it is unlikely that they will ever be read! This being the case I have always thought that I would not have enough to say to justify yet another paperback title. But here I am writing a book about green issues – arguably another commodity which is not in short supply at present!

My reason for writing it is quite simple. For all the media hype about the environment in the last few years and for all the spiritual issues which it has raised, much of Christendom has still not faced with conviction an important question. That is, "How should the Church respond to 'the green decade' of the 1990s"? My own position is that of an evangelical Christian who believes that the so-called "Greens" and the Christian Church have something to learn from one another.

I write with no axe to grind. I do not feel alienated from Christians who believe that the true value of greens is only appreciated on a plate of meat and two veg. Neither do I believe that most Greens are part of a New Age conspiracy to bring in global tree-worship. Indeed generally, Greens and Christians have too often been guilty of caricaturing one another.

As I have suggested, there are very many excellent books

which have been written to inform us and to challenge us about the current ecological crisis and to help us make an appropriate response. There are also a number of Christian volumes which bring valuable biblical perspectives to the issues and outline a greener theology. In some small way, I hope that this book will contribute to both these categories without being a load of recycled pulp.

However, my overriding goal in writing this book has been to fill a small gap on the bookshelf. I have attempted to provide something which can easily be read and understood both by any Christian who would not consider themself to be green, and by any Green who would not consider themself to be Christian. I have tried to be as clear, straightforward and light as possible, neither insulting the readers' intelligence nor baffling them with too much jargon and with too many facts.

Given that its scope is therefore broad, I should make some comments about how best to use the book. It is intended not as a factual textbook, but as an argument to stimulate Greens to consider Christ and Christians to consider the environment. I hope that it will make most sense if it is read from cover to cover, but some people may wish to focus on say, the biblical material or practical steps more immediately. For this reason it has been divided into four parts.

Part One, "What's it all about?", examines the reasons why people (whether or not they are Christian) are sometimes turned off the Green movement and provides a thumb-nail sketch of the current crisis. The reader who is well-informed and well-convinced about environmentalism may wish to skip this part.

Part Two is entitled, "What does God say?" and introduces the main biblical content of the book. Against the backdrop of the current crisis, it sets out what the Bible tells us about creation, the fall and God's plan of salvation. It concludes by looking at some reasons why the Church has been so slow to develop its own distinctive environmental ethic.

Part Three, "What can I do?", begins with a chapter on the Kingdom of God as the lynch-pin connecting the Church and environmental action. It continues with an overview of some of the basic ways in which Christians can respond to the Green agenda, both in our thinking and practically.

Finally, Part Four comprises a glossary of terms, a resources list and indexes. Each of the last four chapters ends with a section on how to take practical steps.

My hope is that this book shows that a biblical faith is not centred completely around people at the expense of the rest of creation, and that it does not justify an uncaring and destructive worldview. I also hope to show that Christianity makes some sense of the problems of decay and suffering. Best of all, it presents a person who describes himself as the "Alpha and Omega". This means "the Beginning and End" or "First and Last".

Jesus, the Bible tells us, was involved in the creation at the start, he holds it together in the present, and will bring life to its fulfilment and death itself to the grave in the end. This Jesus helps us not only to understand the planet and find hope for the earth, but also to understand ourselves and truly find our place in the universe.

Please do not leave this book on your bookshelf – either read it, pass it to someone who will or recycle it in some other creative way!

A NOTE ON VOCABULARY

Words are fraught with limitations, meaning different things to different people in different contexts. I have included a glossary of terms as an appendix to this book to try to prevent jargon from obstructing the readers' understanding of the subject. However, I would like to make a few comments here.

"Green" is perhaps the vaguest of all words used in the book, and I will allow its full meaning to unfold. However, the word begins with a capital only when referring to people, ie "the Greens". It begins with a small "g" when referring to the concept of green-ness, eg "green movement", "green living", etc.

"Third World" is no longer recognised as a valid category, lumping together too many diverse nations. It has also been seen as being derogatory, implying third class status. I use the phrase only as a shorthand – most people understand that it describes the poorest and least well-developed countries, without suggesting that they are in any way inferior.

"Church" is used with a capital "C" to describe the universal *ekklesia*, or people of God, regardless of denomination. When a small "c" is used I am usually referring to individual local congregations.

"Christian" and "Christianity" both begin with capitals, as do "Moslem", "Islam", "Hindu", and so on.

"Wholistic" is spelt with a "w" to separate it from the more specific idea of "holism". I use the word to describe an emphasis on wholeness rather than on oneness.

I have followed the American words for big numbers: a billion is one thousand million and a trillion is one thousand billion.

I have tried to avoid exclusive language wherever possible, using "humanity" or "people" instead of "man", "humankind" instead of "mankind" and so on. I hope that this does not prove too clumsy or tiresome for the reader.

Unless otherwise stated, Bible references are quoted from the New International Version published by the International Bible Society, 1979.

Factual information in this book stopped at 1 January 1992.

PART ONE

WHAT'S IT ALL ABOUT?

Chapter 1

CRISIS – WHAT CRISIS?

Why People are Turned Off the Green Movement

There is simply no argument about it: Planet Earth is not well at present. What we have come to describe as environmental destruction continues relentlessly and seemingly plumbs new depths every year. After the ozone hole, Chernobyl and the Exxon Valdez, 1991 brought a new spectre. As the Iraqi leader, Saddam Hussein, released millions of barrels of crude oil into the Persian Gulf, the world faced "environmental terrorism". Some problems can be mopped up painstakingly – others are even harder to solve.

In the light of this state of affairs, what seems remarkable is that most people can be horrified, but take little action. I am not trying to send anyone on a guilt-trip – there are some good reasons why this happens. Before taking a snap shot of the present crisis I want to touch on five of these reasons.

1. Spare me the Jargon

Global-warming, acid rain, desertification, air pollution, nuclear contamination, Third World debt, water depletion . . .

You would think that there is hardly a person alive on this planet who does not know that something's going on. If there is anyone in Britain who has never heard words like "environment-friendly", "greenhouse effect" or "phosphate-free" then they deserve the Hermit of the Year award. Meanwhile, the rest of us are awash in a sea of jargon.

I am neither a scientist nor an economist, but it seems that I am constantly bombarded and bamboozled with terms which I did not get the right "A" levels to understand. I am sure that this is quite a turn-off for some people who would otherwise be quite interested and concerned about what we now automatically call "green living" and "green thinking".

Of course, ecology is a science and a little knowledge is a dangerous thing. Non-scientists using scientific terms can find themselves in pretty hot water. However, common-sense, a genuine concern for the environment and a readiness to change are surely more important than a physics degree. At the end of this book you will find a glossary of terms (Appendix 1) with some (hopefully) simple descriptions of some difficult and complex words and phrases.

2. What's the score?

Another turn-off is that it seems very hard to know whether or not you've got your facts right. I think of my friend, Keith, who was concerned about the cruel farming of battery hens. He had decided to start eating free-range eggs when another friend, Dwayne, told him, "its all a con – free-range hens are kept outside, but there's 3,000 of them per acre!" Depressed and confused, Keith just gave up and went back to so-called "fresh farm eggs".

There is often the same sort of confusion about recycled paper, green-labelling and degradable plastics. Information is power and statistics can be used to create some strange myths. After all, it has been said that a statistician is somebody who sees a person with their head in the oven and their feet in the fridge and says that on average they are very comfortable!

On the other hand, some people might have their doubts about the facts presented by environmental groups. Don't they tend to over-react? . . . Are they reliable? . . . Don't they have an "axe to grind"? . . . The cynical motto, "Don't believe what you read" seems to be the safest policy!

Unfortunately, if you really want to get your facts right there is no short-cut around doing some homework of your own. The subjects of today's environmental debates are tomorrow's firm facts. Some years ago there were rows about whether or not saturated fats in food, lead in petrol or CFC's in aerosols are really harmful. In the end, people have been convinced and adjustments have been forced upon producers as purchasers have voted with their feet and with their cheque-books.

If you want to know the facts about an issue, look into it. Everyone will be falling over themselves to give you the information. Read and listen to what both sides have to say and make up your own mind. Ask yourself, "Who has most to gain; who has most to lose?" See Appendix Two at the end for some names, addresses and some hot-tips on how to go about making enquiries.

3. The Ostrich syndrome

Referring back to my earlier story, it is easy to become a Keith and give up. Many people think that they might as well imitate the panic of the ostrich, bury their heads in the sand and leave it all to the "experts". Sadly, this will not do. There is no miracle cure or quick fix to our problems. The ecological crisis is *our* problem, a problem of global scale but of significance to every individual. It is disturbing for some to face the fact that each of us bears responsibility for our impact on the planet.

But if your idea of a true Green is somebody who is harmless to the natural world, squeaky clean and worthy of an environment-friendly label of their very own – think again. For a start, none of us are phosphate-free! In fact, phosphates are a mineral vital to our nutritional intake and a major component of our bones. Equally, the careless discharge of human sewage has had a poisonous effect on our rivers and coasts. It has long been understood and accepted that human life is polluting and consuming by its very existence.[1]

Some people will want to be ostriches about the current situation because of its complexity. There is no denying that thinking about the ecological crisis will make your brain hurt a bit. But think we must. To start "seeing green" is more than just jumping on a bandwagon, it prevents us becoming dinosaurs – heading clumsily for extinction.

My son, Sam, likes to be read the story book of Aesop's Fables. These simple but profound animal parables can speak clearly about our human behaviour. Let me remind you of the Grasshopper and the Ant.

> One summer's day a grasshopper was dancing in the sun. He saw a tiny ant hurrying by. She looked very tired and hot. "Why are you working on such a lovely day?" asked the grasshopper. "I'm collecting corn for the winter," said the ant. "You should do the same yourself." "I'm enjoying the summer" laughed the grasshopper. I "can't think about winter." The ant went on her way. She joined all the other ants carrying food to their store.
>
> When winter came and snow was on the ground, the grasshopper had nothing to eat. He was so hungry he begged the ants to give him some food. "We worked all summer to collect our corn. What were you doing then?" said one of the ants. "I was busy dancing," cried the grasshopper. "If you can dance all summer and do no work," one ant said crossly, "then you must starve in the winter."[2]

It is not hard to draw the comparison between the Grasshopper – enjoying a life of plenty in the summer whilst ignoring the oncoming winter – and our present consumer society. Perhaps God will not let us perish completely like the Grasshopper in this story, but we ignore the fact that our "summer" cannot last forever at our peril.

Follow that dinosaur?

However we understand the origins of humanity, most people would agree that we have a great ability to adapt. It is logical to suggest that if we are willing to make changes now, then maybe we can avert some of the ecological catastrophes which have been predicted.

I mentioned dinosaurs earlier. Their world changed around them through no direct fault of their own. They could not adjust and perished. We face changes which we have largely caused and which we can both moderate and adjust to. Whether the stakes are the survival of the human race, or just the health and happiness of millions of the world's poor *and* the non-human creation, we *can* make a difference. I am not saying that self-preservation is the best motivation for being responsible – but self-preservation is surely better than self-destruction!

4. In at the deep end

Another turn-off is the scale of the crisis. The global impact and massive size of such issues as the ozone holes and the deforestation of the Amazon Basin can leave us numbed by a feeling of helplessness. If you are like me, watching television pictures of famine in Africa, floods in Bangladesh or refugees in Kurdistan is a traumatic experience. I am sure that this alone does not qualify me for the Nobel Peace Prize – similar thoughts are shared by millions.

But looking in on the actual suffering is only a part of the trauma. I hoof off to the Bank with my tenner for the latest appeal, but somehow I have a nagging doubt. Has the money done more for my conscience than for a suffering African person? Will any aid really get through? Have I made a difference at all?

Well, I probably have, but it's sometimes hard to believe. Exactly the same is true of environmental action, particularly of the personal kind. Does my cycle-ride to the office truly reduce the impact of global warming? The phrase "a spit in a bucket" sounds like extravagant exaggeration! If I write to my MP about sewage pumped into the English Channel and lumps of oil on Bognor beach, will he really leap into action in defence of the Sussex coast? "Look – a pink elephant flying past the window", I hear you retort.

Before we get too depressed let's think about the green credo, "think globally, act locally". You see, the opposite to action is far more depressing. It says that you and I are totally powerless to control our future and our destiny. It says that the forces which work against the well-being of the environment – big business, population growth and plain human greed – are completely unstoppable.

Of all periods in history this should be one when we can muster greater hope than this. When I studied history at school, the political force of communism in Russia and the Eastern Bloc seemed like a huge monolithic giant. No historian worth his salt would dare to suggest how it could be moved. Of course it was not moved – it just got pushed right over! It was not defeated by an enemy, but rejected by its own people. I remember being with Charlotte in a holiday camp chalet and watching TV pictures of the first people to be let through the Berlin Wall. Tears welled up in our eyes as the first symbolic hammer blows began to destroy that infamous barricade to freedom. Romania, Poland, Bulgaria, Hungary, Yugoslavia and, of course, what used to be Gorbachev's Soviet Union soon became part of the same mass movement. All of a sudden the powerless and apparently hopeless people of those regimes had made a difference.

Light a candle

The inspiration behind the pressure group Friends of the Earth, Jonathon Porritt, likes to quote a Quaker proverb. "It is better to light one small candle than to curse the darkness". This brings out another dimension of why the scale of the problem should not discourage us. By starting to act and think in a different way – recycle, re-use, do I need this?, etcetera – our attitude changes. We look at the world in a far more wholistic way and this has a knock-on effect.

Why has the "environment-friendly revolution" hit our societies? As I mentioned earlier, it is because attitudes have been changing that pressure has been brought to bear and because of this manufacturers, retailers and governments have been forced to make a response – however flimsy some may consider it.

Certainly for a Christian, to "light a candle" is a wholly reasonable idea. For we know that God has called us to be light in his world.

5. Apathetic haze

The final turn-off is apathy. As the saying goes, "I used to be apathetic, but now I can't be bothered"! Sadly, in our culture most people are indifferent about most things. Show too much commitment to something or too much passion on a subject and you're likely to be branded a fanatic! We don't like to hold principles too firmly because compromise is a way of life for us. "Live and let live" might be the justification for our attitudes, but it leads to live and let die.

It saddens me that so many people would prefer to take a cheap swipe at the green movement rather than listen to what it has to say. Whether it's a "knee-jerk" response that lumps nearly all environmentalism with the New Age movement or a patronising comment about muddle-headed idealism, many people are dismissive of the real issues so that they don't have to be troubled by them.

Jesus tells a relevant story in the twelfth chapter of Luke's gospel. It is the parable of the Rich Fool.[3] Having provided for himself well, a certain rich man relaxed and said to himself,

> " 'Take life easy; eat, drink and be merry'. But God said to him, 'You fool! This very night your life will be demanded from you. Then who will get what you have prepared for yourself?' "

Just as the story of the Grasshopper and the Ant teaches us not to run away from an approaching crisis, so this parable teaches a similar lesson. That is, if we enjoy comfort and security then we should be asking ourselves the hard question, "How does God want me to use this wealth?"

The reality of the situation is that the comfort and comparative wealth which we all enjoy in the West are largely built on the suffering of others and on the pillaging of the planet. Some people will dodge the information which makes the extent of the problem so plain. Others will distort it or suggest that Greens are getting hysterical. If you want to stay comfortable – to "eat, drink and be merry" without thought for those who are hungry, thirsty and despairing – don't read on. But I hope you will, because you can be part of the solution, and not just part of the problem.

Summary

I have sought to identify five things which turn people off seriously considering green issues: technical jargon, difficulty in knowing who to believe, the complexity of the ecological crisis, the scale of that crisis and apathy.

There are probably many other reasons. Greens can come across as a little humourless and untrendy – tweed jackets, C&A slacks and open-toed sandals with socks underneath are not unheard of.

Then, of course, there is the crank factor. I'm afraid that some people might actually think that too much green-thinking can render you a couple of sandwiches short of the full picnic! If Greens could only shake off their slightly cranky image, they would certainly win more supporters.

There may be other doubts and questions which Christians would raise from a theological position. I want to consider these later, but for now, I hope I have shown that we cannot afford to look at the green agenda with preconceived ideas. Let us be willing to lay aside our prejudices and take a look at some facts.

Notes

1. Pollution has been described as putting the balance of nature into imbalance.
2. "Animal Stories" - Watson & Price, Usborne Publishing Ltd., 1982.
3. Luke 12:13–21.

Chapter 2

ONE GIANT LEAP BACKWARDS . . .

The Ecological Crisis

An Iceberg's Ugly Tip

Picture this: an open-cast coal mine with surrounding countryside pocked with excavations. Huge slag-heaps rising like monstrous zits on the horizon, the air rank with the gassy odours of the mining process.

When we notice England's "green and pleasant land" suffering rape and pillage under industry, road building and intensive farming, it is easy to get indignant. Outrage comes cheap towards these blots on the landscape.

But so often we fail to realise that we are seeing and smelling no more than the tip of the proverbial iceberg. It is precisely because one bit of environmental vandalism nearly always sets in train a series of domino effects that the overall picture is indeed an ecological crisis. In this chapter I want to try to take a snap shot of this crisis. I want to use a wide-angled lens – not to focus on too much detail, but on the big picture.

A Rolex with a Difference

God has made an incredible and truly wonderful earth – how it works so well is hardly believable and fills us with wonder. The elements of earth, water and atmosphere are delicately linked by a number of different cycles – the cycles of life. The way that they hold together so perfectly is often likened to the workings of an infinitely complicated clock. Many of us shudder at such a mechanical illustration of a world which is so alive, but one thing's for sure – it's a mighty compliment to the clock-maker!

We all take so much of it for granted. Let's think of something as simple as oxygen – essential for every breath that we breathe. The atmosphere's perfect balance of oxygen, nitrogen, carbon and other gases is only maintained because God has built recycling into life. We convert our oxygen into carbon dioxide (CO_2), whilst through the process of photosynthesis plants absorb CO_2 and release oxygen. All very clever.

In fact, all forms of plant and animal life are constantly recycling different gases and minerals to make them available for another form of life. You could say that cycles are as important in nature as they are in the Tour de France. Vegetation is eaten by small animals, and small animals by larger animals. These die and decompose, releasing their compounds and minerals to provide nutrition for plant life again.

Of course, we all know that life is never quite that simple! God didn't want us to work it all out and get bored. The Venus fly-trap, for example, throws my neat little description of life-cycles into absolute chaos – but the processes still go on.

How Fragile We Are

The point is that God has created the earth with a very fine ecological balance. Humankind has a unique power to make drastic changes to its environment – like draining the wet places and irrigating the dry – and so to upset this balance. Careless pollution in one place often hurts our world somewhere down the line – out of sight and usually out of mind. Sometimes our technological advances can be one small step for part of humanity, but one giant leap backwards for the whole creation.

In the last chapter, I wrote of our essential ability as people to adapt. Scientists tell us of wide global temperature fluctuations over thousands and, some would say, millions of years. If this is true, then many forms of life have survived and adapted to dramatic changes. This argument is often quoted to divert attention away from gloomy environmental forecasts.

As we look at humanity's impact on the planet, it is important to try to understand how this impact is being felt in different areas and what changes these involve. Whether or not they are changes that can be survived, few are changes for the better.

1. Land impoverished

What a Wonderful World

If you believe that everything has evolved by pure chance, how lucky we are in the way that the world has turned out by the random process of natural selection! If you believe in a personal creator God, how generous, creative and inventive is his handiwork. Different climate zones, different altitudes, different bed rocks. Different textures, different tastes, different shades of green (not to mention different shades of Greens!) All of which gives the one third of the world's surface covered by dry land a glorious wealth of variety.

So far I have visited only two of the world's continents, but it is amazingly easy to find something new in the natural environment everywhere. New sounds, new sights, new smells; new trees, new animals, new landscapes. How different are the rolling steppes of Kansas from the drumlins of southern Sweden; the tropical Flamingo from the Snow Goose.

Ignoring for a moment the planet's animal life, I want to consider first humanity's impact upon the vegetation which so richly covers the earth, and the soil which supports it.

The Great Green Globe

The earth's surface is remarkably well-off for plant life. In fact, there are very few areas which could properly be described as inhospitable. Before the radical interference of man, at least sixteen distinct areas of natural vegetation existed – from mountainous slopes and tundra to dry tropical scrub and desert.[1] But now in Western Europe, human activity has so altered the natural plant cover that virtually nowhere does it exist in its original form.

If you have ever wondered why there is so much fuss about the tropical rain forest, think for a moment about the humble tree. It holds a place of special importance in the ecological balance of the earth. Trees clean the air, conserve the soil, maintain its fertility, store water, provide a habitat for wildlife and play a vital role in regulating the climate. What's more, they provide a source of fodder for animals and fruit, fibres, firewood and timber for man.

Globally, it is thought that forests have shrunk from 6 billion hectares to 4 billion hectares (that is, by 30%) in the past 10,000 years.[2] In temperate zones, on top of the centuries of human population growth which lead to the cutting down of forest for agricultural land, there are the new problems of air pollution and particularly of acid rain.[3]

However, since 1945, attention has focused on the tropical rain forests, which have been destroyed at an alarming rate. If the present rate of destruction continues, half the remaining tropical rain forest will disappear by 2020.[4] The importance of this disaster can hardly be exaggerated. The loss of forests is closely linked to such issues as global warming, climatic change, air pollution, desertification, floods, species extinction and the rights of indigenous peoples.[5] As with most environmental problems, it is the poor who suffer the worst effects.

Brazil

The roots of this disaster are often deep, complex and tragic. A look at the story of Brazil gives us some idea of this. When the Portuguese reached Brazil around the year 1500, it is estimated that there were about 7 to 8 million Indians in 200 tribes in the Amazon region. By 1960, Brazil's population had grown to 70 million with an extra two million being added each year. The richest 5% of the population lived in luxury, whilst the rest lived in hideous shanty towns. The military government and the World Bank came up with a ripping wheeze of a solution. If the Amazon basin could be developed, the landless could be moved from the drought-stricken grasslands. Then the forest could be cleared to grow food and cash crops for export.[6]

The problem is that after 30 years have gone by, and $2.9 billion has been spent, a chunk of rain forest twice the size of Switzerland has been lost forever. What's more, it has provided less than 500 real permanent jobs and has still left Brazil a net importer of beef! 95% of the 17 million people who had hoped for a better life swelled the population of the shanty towns. Worse still, 187 tribes have now disappeared. Their cultures have been lost forever and, with them, knowledge of how to live sustainable lifestyles in the region.[7]

Before we raise our hands in abject shock and horror, have a quick look at your replacement front door or your attractive wooden salad bowl. The timber traders may have an armful of excuses, but the fact is that the world's largest importer of tropical mahogany is – Great Britain and Northern Ireland. Worth asking a few telling questions of your local DIY superstore, perhaps?

Soil Erosion

Deforestation is only one of the pressures facing the earth's land surface. The expanding world population, particularly in the Third World, means that more and more land gets taken out of the rural economy. More people are trying to live off the same land. The result? An area of vegetation larger than the size of Scotland is destroyed every year and soil erosion threatens one third of the world's land surface.[8]

Soil is another of those vital, but vulnerable quantities in the ecological equation. The cycles of life take place between the elements of dry land, water, air and the animals and vegetation which live on earth. As far as the dry land is concerned, its life is sustained almost entirely by the 6–10 inches of topsoil which covers most of the earth's surface. Over long stretches of geological time, soil has been formed at a faster rate than it has been eroded, to build up this rich life-supporting layer.

More recently, deforestation, over-grazing and the spread of agriculture due to rising populations have reversed this trend. In the United States, a 1982 survey showed that more than 2 billion tons of topsoil was being lost in excess of new soil formation. Around the world, this figure is estimated at 26 billion tons of soil washed and blown away each year.[9]

Continual erosion gradually bleeds the land of its natural productivity. In turn, the land fails to offer support for the peoples who depend upon it. Over the past ten years, our hearts have been touched by pitiful scenes of misery and we have put our hands in our pockets for Live Aid, Band Aid and Comic Relief – and rightly so. But "aid", while essential for short-term disasters, is only a very small part of the solution. It is the tangled problems of Third World debt, deforestation, soil erosion and the consequent spread of deserts which lie at the root of the land's poverty in tropical areas.

These factors in turn have contributed to the repeated tragic famines in Ethiopia and other areas near the Sahara. They are not truly "natural disasters" as they are often described. Rather there is an on-going environmental disaster – mostly of our making – which natural forces only reveal more clearly.

Not Quite Ambridge

A little closer to home, and on a slightly smaller scale, there are many other threats to the land and to its plant-life. The CPRE[10] tells us that an unspoilt area the size of Berkshire, Bedfordshire, Buckinghamshire and Oxfordshire has been "paved-over" or disappeared under concrete in the last 40 years.[11] Today, like never before, our countryside is in a state of siege.

As far as the land still under farming is concerned, the

siege just takes a different form. Most of us "townies" in Britain probably still have a slightly romantic view of the countryside and of farming. In fact it is now more like a high-tech industry!

Increasingly, crops are being specialised by selective breeding and more recently by genetic modification. They are designed to respond to artificial fertilisers, pesticides, machine-harvesting, transportation and so on. The dangers of this include a loss of the diversity of crops, with their various strengths and weaknesses. This loss could be catastrophic if the few selected species suffer from an epidemic or from other adverse conditions.

Then there is the bizarre European Common Agricultural Policy. Despite the Community's high level of self-sufficiency in food, processes which strain the land to increase production are still encouraged. There seems something amiss when consumers have to pay 1% of their VAT to cover the cost of storing surpluses and shoppers pay an extra £5 each week on food bills to maintain prices at an artificially high level.[12] This begins to appear grossly immoral in the context of 730 million hungry people in the world.[13]

The way in which this over-production is secured is often through high levels of chemical use, particularly nitrates and phosphates in fertilisers and toxins in pesticides. There is real concern that up to 64% of pesticides applied to wheat may end up, unaltered, in bread.[14]

Nitrates, which easily dissolve and wash into the rivers and groundwater reduce oxygen and so damage our fresh water. Further, one and a half million Britons are exposed to nitrate levels in water which exceed the maximum EEC limits.[15] This may contribute to oxygen deficiency in babies and to cancer in adults.

I'm afraid that all this is a long way from our cosy images of an idyllic Ambridge-type farming life. I don't want to be accused of sentimental nostalgia – my ancestors were farm labourers until the Agricultural Depression of the 1820s drove them to the granite quarries – for even at the start of this century the lot of the farm worker was a hard and unromantic one. Long hours, back-breaking labour and poor housing were routine – and imagine farm work before welly boots!

Neither do I want to be accused of bashing the farmers (or for that matter the industrialists) as if they should take all the blame. It is us – the consumers – who make demands on the producers and perhaps care too little about how they are met. If we are all part of the problem we must all seek to be part of the solution. Perhaps a check in the mirror to attend to the planks in our own eyes should come before eagerly looking for specks in others'.

Nonetheless, modern agriculture provides a familiar scenario – whilst improved technology offers opportunities for greater comfort, profit and productivity, it has also led to greater destruction of the natural environment. This is supported by survey after survey. For example, one in 1987 revealed that nearly 37% of agricultural land in England and Wales is subject to a "higher than acceptable degree" of soil erosion.[16]

Agriculture apart, land is also impoverished by many other sorts of pollution. Rubbish tips, dumped poisons, broken cars, thrown away cans and dropped wrappers are all symptoms of our waste and carelessness. Some just look ugly, others can hurt.

I remember well my sister and I playing in an open-air swimming pool in Harlow when we were both under ten. Whilst running around the edge of the pool, Sarah trod on the neck of a broken glass bottle, cutting a deep gash into the arch of her foot. She needed several, very painful stitches. I recall her screams and how I felt about those who had carelessly caused her needless pain. It was, for me, a small window into the global suffering we all cause.

2. Water impoverished

Water, water everywhere but not a lot to drink!
Apologies to Samuel Taylor Coleridge for butchering his

famous poem, "The Rime of the Ancient Mariner". Today, it is not just those staring at undrinkable sea-water that may utter this cry. Water covers three-quarters of the world's surface (it also constitutes nine tenths of human body volume) yet only 2% of this mass is fresh water and most of it is locked up in the polar ice caps.[17] In 1980 the Brandt Report stated that "lack of safe water is a major cause of ill-health; in virtually half the world, water supplies are uncertain".[18] That which is available is suffering serious depletion in a variety of distinct ways. Different pressures apply in different areas – in the Third World it is scarcity; in the industrial world it is quality.

The following brief account amply shows us the extent of the first situation:

> "Swaminathan Asokan dreams of water. He sees it gushing out of a giant tap. He watches it filling bucket after bucket. He savors [sic] its coolness. Then he wakes up to a nightmare. For at his house in Madras, India's fourth largest city, there is no water: the tap has long been dry. So he gets up in the dark of night and, laden with plastic pails, takes a five minute walk down the street to a public tap. Since the water there flows only between 4 and 6 a.m., Asokan, a 34-year-old clerk at a finance company, tries to be in line by 3.30 a.m. His reward: five buckets of water that will have to last the day.
>
> Compared to many of his countrymen, Asokan is fortunate. Thousands of Indian villages have no local water supply at all . . .[19]

Statistics for water supply, as with other environmental hot potatoes, are often depressing: of the 40,000 children who die each day, most are victims of diarrhoea and other side effects of the water crisis; in Peking, a third of the wells have gone dry; thanks to disastrous land management the Aral Sea in Russia has shrunk by two-thirds in the past 30 years. Again, increased population must carry much of the blame. The hydrological cycle cannot keep up with the amounts of water required for domestic and industrial use.

Even in areas where rainfall is plentiful, the quality of water is deteriorating. I referred above to the water pollution indirectly caused by farming, especially by nitrates and pesticides. Some pollution is more direct, with many towns pouring sewage straight into rivers virtually untreated.

Industry, once again, is a major culprit. About one-fifth of the world's chemical production takes place on the banks of the River Rhine. Nonetheless, 20 million Europeans still obtain their drinking water supplies from the river. Cornelius van der Veen, head of the Dutch water works in the Rhine catchment area, is quoted as saying "Even well-thought-out purification and reprocessing systems mean that just about every substance present in untreated water is also found in drinking water".[20] Readers in the UK should not feel too relieved not to be Dutchmen: 83% of us drink water which has passed through waste water treatment plants!

Of course, the sea can cope with only so much dumping as well. When on holiday in Greece a few years ago, my wife cut her foot on a hidden rock whilst swimming in the beautiful, clear blue Mediterranean Sea. We were surprised that the wound got infected and did not heal at all. We were more surprised when we were told by our GP back in England, "this is quite common, the Med. is so full of chemicals you should never go into the water with a cut"!

Greenpeace warned in 1987 that the North Sea could be irreversibly damaged within five years if pollution was not controlled. In 1984 it received 5,570,000 tonnes of industrial waste and 5,100 tonnes of sewage sludge. Bear that in mind before you next go for a dip in Skegness!

3. Air impoverished

All I need is the air that I breathe.

Each of our senses gives us a unique reference point to judge what is going on around us. So even though air is invisible, and even though much of what is going into the air is invisible, we can often taste, smell and even hear the pollution which is filling our world.

Many readers (though not the author!) will remember the phenomenon of "smogs" which plagued Britain's cities before the Clean Air Act of 1956. This very early piece of environmental law created smokeless zones and has removed an obvious and unpleasant form of air pollution. Smog (which is still alive and well in other parts of the world) is a foul combination of smoke from the burning of coal, mixed with fog. The ugly mixture can be readily smelt, felt, seen and tasted. In the 1940s and 1950s it allowed damp, polluted air to cloak cities like London, sometimes for days and often with hundreds or thousands of deaths resulting.

Today, London smog may be a memory, but air pollution is not. Everyone has now heard of acid rain – the most publicised form of air pollution over the past decade. I mentioned acid rain earlier in this chapter with reference to deforestation. Closely related to industry as it is, the main effects of acid rain are away from the tropics. By 1986, no fewer than half the forests of the Netherlands, Switzerland and West Germany showed signs of damage.[21] All European forests are now affected to some degree.

Through air pollution, chemical stresses are passed into the soil and in some areas replanting after the death of damaged trees is impossible. So deforestation through air pollution can often mean that re-forestation is out of the question for many years.

Blowing in the Wind

Of course, it has long been recognised that air pollution knows no borders and can be very easily exported with the help of tall chimneys and the wind blowing in the right (or rather, wrong) direction. The Scandinavians were the first to point this out in the sixties (although two decades were to pass before evidence showed the link between air pollution, acid rain, chemical changes in the water, dead fish and sickly trees).

It did not take a massive brain to work out that there was

some connection between British power stations, over 1,700 Norwegian lakes with dying fish and a prevailing south-westerly wind!

Other factors, including the fact that little serious burning of fossil fuels is done in Norway, should have left the British government flushed in the cheeks and with their hands in the air. Instead, every step towards cutting air pollution, or better still, exploring alternative energy sources, has been met with the dragged feet of an unwilling child.

The incident which has probably made the greatest impact on the debate recently is the nuclear accident at Chernobyl in the Ukraine, on 26 April 1986. This accident, caused by a deliberate experiment, led to more than thirty immediate fatalities and a deathly cloud of radioactivity which swept westward over northern Europe. Controversy has raged over how many cancer deaths will occur in Europe as a result of Chernobyl. The UK National Radiological Protection Board put the figure at around 1,000, whereas some US experts say that one million would be more accurate.[22] Imagine how this has also affected other forms of life – the plants, trees and animals – and the quality of the soil.

If you were against nuclear power before Chernobyl, you might say that it's an ill wind that blows nobody any good. Many have felt for some time that nuclear power is not a clean form of energy, with disastrous accidents occurring every few years. Surely Chernobyl has now knocked nuclear power firmly on the head for some time. Pessimists, however, say that this will only lead to more burning of fossil fuel and therefore create more air pollution. Since the early 1980s, activities such as generating electricity, driving cars, and producing steel have each year released into the atmosphere over 5 billion tons of carbon, nearly 100 million tons of sulphur and lesser amounts of nitrogen oxides. In addition to damaging trees and lakes, the release of these gases corrodes buildings and is thought to contribute to heart and respiratory disease.

When looking at air pollution, the motor car is often singled out as a particular demon. Ten years ago, campaigning to remove lead from petrol was well under way. True, lead is a very harmful air pollutant and has been strongly linked to problems in children's brain development. However, the marketing men get hold of the issue and we end up with strange messages on advertisements. If you were to believe them, you would think that while you are filling up at the "green pump" you are actually doing the environment a big favour! The latest trick is to repeat the process with the catalytic converter.

Of course, these are small steps in the right direction, but the type of fuel and size of engine are comparatively cosmetic details. The truth of the matter is that every time we switch on the ignition, we start to pollute with a capital "P".

Warm Enough?

Most people are now aware that air pollution is about more than just the air that we breathe. For those of us that only used the word 'atmosphere' when someone opened their mouth and put their feet straight in, our horizons have been broadened. 'Ozone-layer' and 'global-warming' are clichés of our generation. Damage to the earth's atmosphere by air pollution is now rarely contested: most scientists agree that the worst results of our waste could be occurring a few miles over our heads.

All those billions of tons of carbon that are being pumped into the air are beginning to alter the delicate balance of gases which makes the earth such an ideal environment for life. More carbon and fewer trees enhance the natural greenhouse effect and start to change the planet's climate.[23]

If you lived in Britain over the glorious summer of 1990 you might have thought that global warming was generally a good idea. On the other hand, if you lived in the Maldives, none of whose 1,196 islands rises more than 2 metres above sea-level, you might have thought differently. Speaking to the General Assembly of the UN in October 1987, the President of that country described the Maldives as "an endangered nation". What did he mean? He was referring to one of the most worrying projected results of global warming: rising sea-levels.

If the earth's overall temperature is actually rising, then the polar ice-caps will slowly start to melt and as sea temperatures rise, the water will expand. The US Environmental Protection Agency estimates that sea-levels could rise by 1.4 to 2.2 metres by the year 2100.[24] Not only the Maldives, but many coastal mega-cities could be in danger of terminal flooding down the line – New Orleans, Cairo, Shanghai and London.

But rising sea-levels are only one of the anticipated effects of global warming. Agriculture, too, may face similar turmoil. As moisture in the soil during the summer growing season declines, the richest corn-producing land would revert to rough grassland. In turn, grassland would become semi-arid land and what is now semi-arid could drop off the edge and become sterile desert. The cost of this could be measured in many ways – in financial terms alone, the estimated price of irrigation and drainage runs into hundreds of millions of pounds. Of course, areas like Canada, Russia and Argentina may well benefit as climate zones shift northwards – but these are hardly among the world's poorest nations.

Serious Depletion

In the late 1970s, scientists discovered a hole in what is now known universally as the ozone-layer. Although there is still some mystery about it, the ozone-layer is thought to be a protective shield of gases which cuts out harmful ultra-violet (UV) rays from the sun. The hole, over Antarctica, was twice the size of the USA in 1987 and could suggest a thinning of the ozone-layer globally. Other holes have since been found. The results of these nasty UV rays hitting the earth's surface could be eye diseases, falling crop production and an increase of skin cancer.

The much-publicised enemies here are not just burning fossil fuels (although nitrogen oxides are thought not to be ozone's best friends), but the chlorofluorocarbons (CFCs to you and me) which propel aerosols, make foam packaging for junk food and keep our fridges cold. Sometimes being friendly to the environment is not an easy matter. CFCs were good news when they first appeared on the scene, as they did not break down easily and, so it was thought, did not therefore cause any pollution. Unfortunately, CFCs do not break down; they just keep rising into the upper atmosphere until they hit ozone, which they proceed to deplete!

Taking all this together, air pollution is clearly one of the most critical forms of earth-damage around. The impact of this and all other pollution together is . . .

4. Life impoverished

Extinction is Forever

Although there is thought to have been a mass extinction of species during the Ice Age, we are potentially on the verge of something more destructive, and apparently more deliberate in this present era. The wonderful wealth and variety of life which God has created has been reduced in a ruthless way that he surely did not intend. Those creatures which do survive often face a mean, pathetic or endangered existence.

The activities and growth of the human population first of all demands that more land, water and other resources be harnessed. The shrinking tropical rain forests, which are home to a huge share of the diversity of life on earth, are the focus of concern about this latest potential disaster. Many species of plant, bird and animal are lost before they are ever properly discovered. As the forests are pillaged for timber, cultivable land, roads and other developments, the extinction of one fifth of all species by destruction of habitat is a real possibility. Some estimates, based on research in Panama, have suggested that the loss of tropical forests may lead to the extinction of *one third of all the world's species*.[25]

It is not just the loss of the forests which threatens to impoverish the diversity of life on earth: wetlands, coral reefs and heathlands are all sources of this abundant variety.

There is one overwhelming fact about extinction which again has been well exploited by the sloganeers – *extinction is for ever*. For the Madagascar serpent eagle, the Valencia toothcarp and the Moorean viviparous tree snail time is running out – and if it does run out, it's gone forever. There is no virtue in being sentimental, but this is the hard truth.

From a Christian perspective, extinction is much more than just a biological term. It is destroying a creation of our God, whom we will meet. Imagine how you would feel about meeting Leonardo da Vinci if he knew you had set fire to the Mona Lisa!

The situation is slightly less gloomy as far as plant-life is concerned. There is usually the opportunity to save the seeds of threatened plants and trees – but only if they are known about in time. The conservationists are facing the hopeless task of trying to save plants at a fraction of the rate at which they are being lost forever.

Altogether, the IUCNNR,[26] which monitors endangered species, has data on more than 30,000 of these species – 6,000 types of fish, birds, reptiles, etcetera and 25,000 types of flowering plants. Most of these are threatened by the loss of their habitats through human activity.

Another personal window on the crisis: I am a keen birdwatcher, and always eager to see a new species in the wild. I once travelled with friends to the Suffolk/Norfolk border to see a beautiful and rare visitor to Britain – a songbird called the golden oriole. For many reasons, its breeding population has declined and it is now confined to larch trees in the Brecklands. There was still one spot which had always been thought of as a "cert" for finding orioles in Spring. After a long drive through the night, we reached this site at about 4 a.m. one drizzly May morning, all ready to listen out for the fluty dawn song. However, as we progressed along the two mile hike towards the relevant larch woods, we soon realised – there was no larch wood! What used to be many acres of woodland has become many acres of brown corduroy-like ploughed land – another kick in the teeth for conservation.

A Bloody Mess

As far as animals are concerned, those which do survive and are harnessed for human use often face a particularly miserable existence. In bygone days, cruelty to animals was easy to observe and acted as a barometer of a harsher age – pit ponies carrying coal underground in pitch darkness; bulls ripped to pieces by dogs in the "sport" of bull-baiting. Today the "out of sight, out of mind" syndrome means that cruelty is often less obvious. I touched upon factory farming earlier in this chapter as far as it relates to the use of chemicals and the soil. When it comes to the treatment of animals, conditions in factory farms may be fairly described as obscene.

For example, poultry are reared in factories where the average flock size is over 27,000 birds. Layers of hens are crammed together in "chicken cities". Over 95% live in battery cages. Through their diet, lighting and other conditioning, they only exist to produce eggs.

In the early years of our marriage, Charlotte worked for a brief time at an egg-farm and gathered some stomach-churning stories. It was not unusual for the birds to literally turn themselves inside out as they were forced to lay eggs at such an abnormal rate.

The pig has fared little better from the farming revolution. Only 5% of the 750,000 breeding sows in Britain are free-ranged; two-thirds are kept throughout their pregnancies in dry sow stalls with never a glimpse of daylight.[27] In all 3,000 animals are slaughtered in Britain every minute of every day to meet the consumer demand. The conditions in many slaughter houses are widely recognised as appalling.[28]

The situation is no better at sea. Recent scandals have erupted over the routine slaughter of dolphins in the fishing of the tunny which fills our supermarkets with tuna chunks. Before that the clubbing of baby seals in Canada and the butchery which is the whaling industry hit the headlines.

At the time of writing, new concerns are being expressed about drift-netting. This cruelly-effective fishing method involves drift nets up to 64km long which sweep up everything in their path – not only commercial fish but also sharks, dolphins, whales, otters, foraging seabirds – anything that gets in the way. Ecological groups are horrified that this method has been spread by Taiwanese fleets from the Pacific into the Atlantic Ocean. One marine conservationist is quoted as saying, "They will destroy all animal life in the ocean. They will eat up the Atlantic, and then we've had it".[29]

The Poor you will always have . . .

The final way in which life is impoverished by our careless treatment of the environment, is that humanity itself is suffering. Jesus observed that whilst humankind lived for "No. 1", there would always be the rich and there would always be the poor. We have seen already that it is often those that live in the poorest nations of the world which suffer most from soil erosion, deforestation and the spread of deserts. However, there are many other reasons to claim that the poor often pick up the tab for the West's gung-ho approach to the environment.

Pollution is an unavoidable result of human activity and this applies wherever you live. But the kind of pollution which is affecting everyone – particularly global-warming – is produced mostly by rich, industrialised countries. There are two sides to the coin. One side is that the contribution of Third World nations to global-warming, in the shape of greenhouse gas emissions, accounts for only 12% of the world's total. The ability to reduce these emissions is clearly far greater in the developed countries. In addition, the burden of Third World debt owed to Western banks is a major cause of deforestation.[30]

The other side of the coin is that the people who are least able to control pollution – poor people in poor countries – will suffer its most severe consequences. The reason for this is that climate change will most affect those areas which are vulnerable to "natural" problems such as storms, rising sea levels and biological effects on agriculture.

Of course, a rich nations versus poor nations division is far too general and simplistic. There are greedy landowners and industrialists in Third World countries who willingly pollute and destroy habitats to get richer. Likewise, if we stopped importing our mahogany then many labouring loggers in Malaysia and elsewhere would suffer greatly from unemployment. If only life were more straightforward!

Having said this, because in the West we are in the best position to change things, we must take the lead. For example, China's electricity is produced by some of the dirtiest coal-fired power stations in the world. These have been developed partly through aid from Britain.[31] We must cut our own pollution *and* help others to cut theirs.

For Western countries which have been industrialised for two hundred years, it is fine for us now to be environmentally aware. The irony is that we have encouraged Third World countries to industrialise and to develop (everybody wants what we've got) and yet we expect them to learn overnight the lessons which have taken us centuries to learn. Meanwhile, in Asia "sulphurous coal smoke hides a Chinese city from satellite cameras; chemical waste makes Hong Kong's shellfish toxic, potentially lethal; the traffic fumes of Bangkok and Taipei make Los Angeles smell sweet by contrast, and Manila's five main rivers are biologically dead . . ."[32]

In Asia and across the world, all environmental problems are wrapped up with two great causes: population growth and energy use. These are not the root causes, as we will see later, and they are worsened by poverty, corruption and much else. However, all these combine to mean that the human race cannot sustain its present rate of growth and greed for much longer. Action is needed, and the time is now. The earth, our home, is getting poorer and poorer – it is in need of a saviour.

5. Get rich or get it right

Summary
Setting out a catalogue of humanity's folly makes a gloomy beginning to a book and no mistake! It is a gloomy picture but not a hopeless one. Now that the scale of the crisis has been set out, I want to look behind the facts to root causes and to solutions.

For those who really believe that more material wealth can solve the problems of our impoverished planet, the solution is seen to be more economic growth with some ecology tacked on. In other words, keep getting rich. Others see that the solution has got to be more radical. It has got to affect the way we see the world, the way we treat the world and thus the lifestyles that we adopt. Getting more and more growth is less important than getting it right.

In this day of education, communication and information we all know that there are many different philosophies and religions to help us understand the world in which we live. Very few have so far faced up to this question of how to heal the planet.

Buddhism and Hinduism have a high view of animal life, but their quietist cultures contain some of the worst scenes of environmental damage in the world. Paganism, animism and New Age thought see something spiritual in non-human life, but often it is a spirituality of fear, seeking power and domination. Judaism, Islam and Christianity believe in a creator God, but each have regularly failed to demonstrate this in action. Taoism, Confucianism and Humanism all have good intentions to be harmonious with nature but, once again, the facts point in a different direction. The experience of Eastern Europe suggests that Marxism has proved itself to be not only socially and politically bankrupt, but an environmental polluter as well.

Looking into the past will only take us so far. If all world religions, including Christianity, have failed to properly demonstrate a sound environmental ethic in the past, it does not mean that all are equipped to succeed in the future. The basic thesis of this book is that there are many things which Christianity *can* offer as no other faith can. Of all these qualities it is the sense of *wholeness* and *hope* which makes its message a very positive force for change.

In the next section, I want to start at the beginning and see how the Christian message explains the status quo – that is Latin for "the mess we are in now"!

Notes

1 *Times Concise Atlas of the World*, 1982 (after Professor Preston E. James and others.
2 Shell Briefing Service 5, 1990 (SBS5 1990): Forestry in Focus, p8.
3 See Appendix 1.
4 SBS5 1990, p8.
5 Again, see Appendix 1 for more details and explanations of these issues.
6 This project, known as the Polonoroeste regional development programme, was one of many short-sighted, expensive and failed experiments to be undertaken with what was seen as the huge resource of the Amazon Basin.
7 BBCTV The Human Race "Bellamy Rides Again", July 1991.
8 Ibid.
9 Lester R Brown et al *State of the World 1988* Norton, p5.
10 The Council for the Protection of Rural England. Their leaflet was quoted in *The Guardian* 20 June 1988.
11 In addition, 95% of our flower-rich meadows have gone under the plough; 60% of our lowland heaths have been lost; 50% of our ancient woodlands cut down; 50% of our lowland fens drained. On top of all this, 4,000 miles of hedgerows are disappearing each year.
12 Friends of the Earth (FoE) Agriculture.
13 Goldsmith and Hildyard (Eds.) *The Earth Report* Mitchell Beazley, 1988, p90.
14 FoE, ibid.
15 *Earth Report*, p184.
16 Goldsmith and Hildyard (Eds.) *The Earth Report 2* Mitchell Beazley, 1990, p65.
17 World Health Organisation figures.
18 The Brandt Committee North-South: A Programme for Survival The Brandt Committee, 1980.
19 *Time* 5 November, 1990, p45.
20 Quoted in *Earth Report* p82.
21 Lester R Brown et al, ibid., p5.
22 Quoted in *Earth Report* 2 pp38, 39.
23 See Global Warming and Greenhouse effect in Appendix 1.
24 Lester R Brown ibid., p17.

25 *Earth Report* p144.
26 The International Union for the Conservation of Nature and Natural Resources.
27 FoE Agriculture.
28 see chapter 8 for a full quotation on this issue.
29 Quoted in *Time* 27 August, 1990, p35.
30 See World Development Movement *Global Warming and the Third World* 1990, p8.
31 Ibid. p9.
32 *The Economist* 6 October 1990, p21.

PART TWO

WHAT DOES GOD SAY?

Chapter 3

IN THE BEGINNING

Thinking about Creation

Perspective and Truth

The opening four words of the holy writings, or Scriptures, which Christians call "the Bible"[1] are about the most profound words ever written. "In the beginning God". That's how it starts. Before God there was nothing. He was never created, he simply existed. The mystery of eternity, like that of infinity, is beyond the grasp of our limited minds.

When the great Old Testament leader, Moses, asked for the name of this God, so that there would be no confusion when he got home, Moses received an unusual reply, "I AM WHO I AM. This is what you are to say to the Israelites: 'I AM has sent me to you' ".[2] God refuses to submit to our definitions of him – he is the greatest person, thing and event in all reality. He could do anything.

It so happens that God will not do *anything* and *everything*. He has deliberately bound himself by his promises. For example, he has described himself as faithful, so he cannot lie. He has described himself as righteous, so he cannot be evil. He says he is peace and joy, so there is neither disharmony nor depression in his character.

It is so important, having once taken the step to believe in God, that we learn how to see the world as he sees it. The prayer which Jesus taught us to pray begins, "Our Father in heaven".[3] This is more than just a polite way of addressing the Lord; it means that we approach him knowing that whilst we have perspectives on life, he alone has, and is, the truth.

It's only too easy to start from where we are and work backwards to try to understand what God is like. The Bible gives us an opportunity to get it right. We must not define God merely according to what we see, but seek to understand life and everything in it according to God.

This is not the place for going into the many reasons why the Bible should be believed and taken seriously. There are lots of good books which have been written on this subject and – if you are not already convinced – I would recommend that you read one of them.[4] The one thing I am not asking you to do is kiss your brains good-bye!

Hot Potatoes

The whole of the first verse of Genesis chapter one runs like this, "In the beginning God created the heavens and the earth". The fact that God made everything that exists out of nothing is one of the clearest teachings of the Bible.

However, some hot controversies, particularly over the past two centuries, have sometimes prevented more discussion of what the biblical doctrine of creation really means. These have included debates surrounding evolution, the age of the earth and some novel theological ideas to explain God's relationship to the world. Each represents either an attempt by science or philosophy to replace God or the reactions of Christians to these trends. The purpose of this chapter is not to discuss the "how?" questions about creation, but the "why?" questions. Whilst some of these issues are important in themselves, they do not directly relate to a Christian view of the environment, and so fall outside our scope.

Happy Birthday

In contrast to these debates, the Bible does not emphasise the time-scales, the method, or any detailed explanation of the creation. Rather, it tells us about God, about humankind and about our place in the world which he has carefully made.

To the Lord, I believe that the earth is something like the

greatest work of a great artist. It combines the elegance of a sculpture, the beauty of a painting and the drama of a play. On this production, the artist has spared no expense of love, energy and effort. For example, how many shades of red does a sunset need? Yet have you ever looked at the evening sky and thought "if someone painted this, you would call the colours and the features far-fetched!"?

But the earth seems to be more than just a work of art. As a father of two children, I have had the unique privilege of attending the births of both Samuel and Poppy. There can be few human experiences in which so many emotions and thoughts are wrapped up at once – anxiety, pain, relief, unspeakable joy and waves of profound gratitude. (Incidentally, it has been said that atheists' most embarrassing moment is when they feel truly grateful, but have nobody to thank!) The experience of this spectacular event alone is surely enough to bond the feelings of the parent and the well-being of the child forever, although it may be resisted by some.

I do not think that it is sacrilegious to compare this experience, and these feelings, with God's relationship to his created earth. It would be arrogant and unfounded to say that planet earth is, was, or will be the pinnacle of the Lord's creative powers. On the other hand it would be a mistake to view the creation as a hobby which God worked on in the evenings and spare weekends. The way some preachers skip over the subject, one could be forgiven for thinking that our planet home and all it contains was not much more than something which the Lord casually knocked out one afternoon.

Instead, I believe God has invested himself in the creation quite as much as any parent invests themselves in their offspring. The Lord's relations with the earth are infinitely greater than we can understand. Surely God poured himself out in a way similar to a mother bringing children into being. Indeed, some argue that in bringing forth the creation we gain a glimpse of the "femaleness" contained in the Godhead.[5]

God made the earth, and like a watching parent, has stayed involved with it. Indeed, in the New Testament Paul writes that "all things were created by him and for him . . . and in him all things hold together."[6] It is amazing to think that the Lord himself still enjoys the universe he has made. The statement, "And the Lord saw that it was good" is repeated six times in the first chapter of Genesis. One of those was a "very good",[7] which he applied after the making of humanity, showing that people completed the wholeness and goodness of God's creative work.

After all this time, he still is pleased with a blustery autumn day, a rose in the desert, an arctic tern flying from the Antarctic to northern lands to breed. Of course, this also means he is pleased when he looks at you and me.

It's in the Book

As we read the Bible it becomes clear that the three persons of the Godhead were all involved in the earth's beginnings. The actual work of creation is usually thought to belong to the Father, who takes the initiative in the Trinity.[8] However, it was the "Spirit of God" who was "hovering over the waters" when the earth was "formless and empty",[9] and as we have just seen, Christ was also involved as "the Word" of God.[10]

When looking through the Bible to find out more about the creation, we find that it is the Psalms which hold some of the richest of material. Although the contents of the Psalms are largely devoted to worship and adoration of what God has done, there are also some stunning theological statements. "The earth is the Lord's and everything in it".[11] He made it and still owns it. On this one verse, all human pretensions to supremacy are shattered.

We are also given some detailed insights. In Psalm 50 we read,

> ". . . for every animal of the forest is mine,
> and the cattle on a thousand hills.

I know every bird in the mountains,
and the creatures of the field are mine."

This is mirrored in the teaching of Jesus when he says that not one sparrow falls to the ground without God's knowledge;[12] that God clothes the "grass of the field" with more splendour than Solomon in his best "glad-rags";[13] and that the birds of the air are fed by our "heavenly Father".[14]

Meditation on the wonder of God's handiwork has inspired some of the finest recorded praise. Psalm 104 is a matchless song of worship drawn from observing what the Lord has made. From the phrase, "He set the earth on its foundations; it can never be moved",[15] it goes on to describe waterfalls, valleys, wine, trees, thunder, the moon, lions roaring and the sunrise – a vast wealth and variety of splendid creativity. If you have a Bible handy, why not read this Psalm now. Indeed, when you next walk in the country, go alone and take a look at what you see, reflecting upon God as its imaginative maker.

I once did this in a remote valley in central Wales. Above the green valley-floor with scattered oaks and sheep, where redstarts flashed ahead of me and butterflies surrounded me, ravens wheeled over the crags a thousand feet high. The landscape was etched and marked by the glaciers of ancient millenia, which God also made. I could not escape the wonder which the Psalmist expressed – that the God who made this and everything else, made me, loves me and likes me – "Praise the Lord, O my soul!"[16]

An Intricate Web

Of course, there are many aspects of the earth's design about which the Bible is less clear. Sometimes we have to observe with care and clarity. Sometimes other world-views may even give us some insights. For example, one of the best ideas of the New Age movement – and perhaps one of the few with which a Bible-believing Christian can agree – is that there is more unity in the earth than has often been acknowledged.

As we saw in the last chapter, in creating the cycles of life God has made essential links exist between the land, the seas and the atmosphere. Through food chains we observe that nutrients – and pollutants – can be passed from one source to a distant destination. Much of the flavour of Western culture is independence and autonomy. If you look at the created world, it is hard to see anything that is naturally autonomous apart from God himself – and even he is three persons!

We might struggle to explain it – even with the Bible open in front of us – but it is clear that there is life in the earth which is greater than the sum total of the parts. Many people tend to view Christians as rather naive for believing a biblical account of creation. I am not denying that it takes faith to understand that the universe was formed at God's command, so that what is seen was made out of absolutely nothing.[17] The New Testament letter to the Hebrews states exactly this (chapter 11, verse 3).

However, surely it takes as much, if not more faith, to believe that these fine connections which tie us all in with the one planet, have their origins in some sort of inter-stellar road traffic accident. One wag has commented that the likelihood of an explosion of a star resulting in the infinite wonder of life on earth, is as slim as an explosion in a scrapyard producing Concorde!

Where does it fit?

1. Our Starting Point

Cosmic conundrums aside, we can safely say that the doctrine of creation must be the starting point as any Christian seeks to understand the world around them. If we hurry on to talk about the Fall, about sin and about the saving work of Jesus too soon, we may build our beliefs on a thin foundation.

This doctrine gives the Church many of its key distinctives as against other religions and philosophies. For example, because we believe in a God who was "in the beginning" and before the foundation of the earth, we know that humanity is not the centre of the universe. (It could be argued that God has given us a lesson through creation in that the earth revolves around the sun and not the other way round. Of course the opposite seems to be true from the point of view of an earth-dweller. Is this one of God's little jokes at the expense of our human pride?)

2. Absolutes and Objective Truth

From this fact, we can state that life is not just whatever we experience of it or feel about it.[18] Rather, there *is* such a thing as absolute value, because God is constant and unchangeable. There is also an objective basis for ethics. For example, truth *is* truth and not just a wad of plasticine which can be moulded to fit any particular set of circumstances. Faithfulness means keeping promises – and we have been *made* capable of keeping promises.

3. The Importance of Being Obedient

There is a well-known Christian poster which shows a comically twisted and tangled character looking at a motto above a Bible. It reads "For best results: Follow Manufacturer's Instructions". The moral is that we should read the Bible first to save getting our lives into a tangle.

In the light of creation, it is important to recognise that to disregard our Maker and his commands is not wise. The Bible itself seems to suggest that nature is also a "book of revelation" about God – the two should be read together.[19] For example, how much misery has resulted when the basic social and spiritual laws contained in the ten commandments have been ignored – adultery, murder, rejection of parents, lying, lust and all the rest? If we had obeyed God's clear command for monogomous heterosexual practice would we be living with so much wrecked family life, so many insecure children and with sexually-transmitted diseases?

4. Whose rights?

Creation also says something about a proper measure of value. It is where we must begin to think about human rights, animal rights, and any other rights for that matter. If these do exist then they are surely the rights of the Creator – "all things were made by him and for him". As far as humanity is concerned, this has implications for subjects like education (how can we enable each person to become all they were created to be?). It also has implications for politics and economics, for people are not statistics, economic units or lumps of protoplasm. Belief in the unique created value of every individual must also affect the ways in which we treat every person we meet on a daily basis.

As our values are challenged, it should also give some perspective to our wanton consumption and destruction of the earth's non-human resources. Does he want the abundant forests to become sterile deserts? If the Lord knows about every sparrow as it falls, imagine how he feels when a whole species is wiped out! Extinction is forever because God will not start again – he is not in the habit of casual creation. All life is unique and, in a sense, is unrepeatable.

5. Is Nature our Mother?

Further, a doctrine of creation must affect our view of nature as a whole. The fashion is for concepts which deify nature – or "Mother Nature" - and have their roots in pantheism.[20] In other words, nature has become a substitute for God himself.

To be clear about where nature fits is essential in our culture, where different ways of understanding the spiritual character of the world compete. Nature itself does not exist by its own power, but is sustained, like all things, by "the powerful word" of God's Son.[21] However, nature is made by God, essentially good and is one of the major means by which he has revealed himself. As we have seen, through the creativity and the energy of birth he brought it into being.

What is more, it seems that the Creator has woven a number of pictures and lessons into nature from which we humans can benefit. Think of the spider and the fly – how important it is to look where we are going(!), and how easily we can get trapped and caught by life's temptations. Consider the robin, so attractive with its red breast, but quite a bounder underneath – not everything is as lovely as it looks. Or what of the caterpillar and the butterfly, the cygnet (or ugly duckling of nursery rhyme fame) and the swan? Both show that God can work remarkable transformations – and that we should not be discouraged by unpromising beginnings!

6. Creation and Christ

So, the doctrine of creation is key to a right understanding of the basics of reality. However, critical as it is to see God as "creator" from a biblical perspective, it can never be seen as his final revelation. By gazing on a mountain landscape or looking up on a starry night into the "heavenlies", it would be quite possible to be intimidated by such a God. How could he possibly know me or be involved with me? The answer is that he does and is, and proves it in Jesus – the ultimate self-revelation of God. To our amazement he shows to us an infinitely involved God who is both our heavenly Father and our Saviour.

Creatures or Gods?

Having taken a broad view of creation, I now want to look at some of the more specific questions which it needs to answer.

Firstly, where do we humans fit into the bigger picture? As far as scripture is concerned, one can observe two main distinctions. First and foremost, it is essential to state that there is a separation between the Creator and his creatures. Particularly in the light of pantheistic ideas which do not distinguish between God and what he has made, this truth must be held with clarity. It means that all life, human and non-human, originates and owes its continual existence to God himself. This is why Paul can say that,

> ". . . neither death nor life, neither angels nor demons, neither the present nor the future, nor any powers, neither

> height nor depth, nor anything else in all creation, will be able to separate us from the love of God that is in Christ Jesus our Lord" [22]

It is also why the gospels affirm that,

> "Through him all things were made. Without him nothing was made that has been made".[23]

The fact of God's sovereignty over all creation, including humanity, means that nothing is ultimately out of his reach. This is restating the first thought of this chapter – "In the beginning God". There is only God the "I AM", the Creator, and then the rest of the universe – galaxies of stars, planets, ants, gnus, bacteria, Joe Bloggs, you (dear reader) and me – we are all his creatures.

Special creatures

Having made this fundamental distinction, it must not be denied that people have a special character and a special role in creation. This should not be overstated. A careful look at Genesis 1 shows that before the advent of humankind in verse 26, the earth was almost complete. Not only was there day and night, water and dry land, but the vegetation was fruitful (v. 12), the fish and "every moving thing with which the water teems" had been blessed and, again, made fruitful (vv. 21, 22) and the land had produced all kinds of "living creatures" (v. 24). There can be no doubt that in its original state the earth and the life which it supports was by no means dependent upon *humanity* for its existence and its fruitfulness, although it has always remained dependent upon the continuing involvement of a loving *God*.

But the verse which introduces the making of humankind, also introduces a distinction amongst the creatures of the universe. The fact is that this particular aspect of creation is not just unique (which applies to everything), but operates on a unique dimension. Whilst God has invested himself in all that has been made, he has chosen humanity to represent him and to reflect him to the rest of creation:

> Then God said, "Let us make man in our image, in our likeness, and let them rule . . . over all the earth . . ." So God created man in his own image, in the image of God he created him; male and female he created them.[24]

If, in "greening" our view of Christianity and the world, we lose this concept, we are in peril. By reducing humanity to the level of the rest of creation, we are not thinking wholistically, but seriously off the wall! It is not that *homo sapiens* just happens to have emerged from the primeval slime and clawed its way to the top of the evolutionary ladder. Neither does the theological argument for the unique place in creation which humankind alone holds rest upon a claim to be the highest, most intelligent or most developed life-form around. Rather, it rests upon the *means* by which we have been made, and the *relationship* that we still share with God.

To take this further we must turn to the second chapter of the book of beginnings. Genesis 2 provides an expanded view of the two verses explaining the creation of humankind set out above from Genesis 1,

> ". . . the Lord God formed the man from the dust of the ground and breathed into his nostrils the breath of life, and the man became a living being." [25]

People are material (formed from the dust) and yet spiritual (containing the breath of the Lord God). The angels are spiritual beings, the rest of creation is material – humankind exists as both.

Next, people have a unique relationship to God. In Genesis 1:28,29 and Genesis 2:15 we read of the hand-picked role we have been given in the earth. More of this in a moment. There are also glimpses of this relationship of a more intimate kind. In Genesis 3:8 we read that,

"The man and his wife heard the sound of the Lord God as he was walking in the garden in the cool of the day . . ."

God was looking for man and woman in the garden that he had given to them. He wanted to talk with them and to interact with his friends. This is also true when God next walked the earth. Jesus, in Gethsemane, did not want the company of an angel – he wanted his friends.[26] Abraham was known as a friend of God[27] and there is apparently no way of explaining that people everywhere – Christian or not – have a desire for some form of spiritual expression and relationship.

When we think of people as image-bearers of God, it gives us a fresh perspective on some of the qualities which we take for granted. For example, it is hardly surprising that a Creator-God would invest those who carry his likeness with creative skills and gifts – art, music, drama, design, oratory, invention and spin-bowling all contain indirect expressions of the creative life of God. In the same way, in its created origins, work was not a negative or an oppressive thing. Rather, it too was a creative involvement with nature.

I mentioned earlier that all vegetable and animal life were made and put in place before the arrival of man on the time-space scene. However, Genesis 2 again provides a little extra detail and perspective.

". . . no shrub of the field had yet appeared on the earth and no plant of the field had yet sprung up, for the Lord God had not sent rain on the earth *and there was no man to work the ground* . . ." [28] (my italics)

This tells us plainly that the earth was not quite complete without humanity and without its work to co-operate with the fruitfulness of nature. The outstanding children's book "Wonderful Earth" [29] expresses this with disarming simplicity, "we are a bit like God really". Just as God's creation expresses who he is, so our creative work expresses who we are as individuals and as God's children.

In the light of all this, it is hardly surprising that when God saw the wholeness of the completed earth, with humanity at its pinnacle, he was well pleased and took a day off – "God saw all that he had made, and it was very good." [30]

Vandalising Eden

The second question which a doctrine of creation must answer concerns man's relationship with non-human life. The truly biblical position on this matter has long been misunderstood, both within the Church and outside it. Because of this, the Christian faith has been blamed for creating a "grey" (perhaps "red" would be more appropriate) as opposed to a green way of thinking about animals, and about the rest of the environment. Green Christians are often put on the defensive about this issue, but I believe that a robust defence must be made against some incorrect accusations.

No passage in the bible has drawn more criticism from Greens than Genesis 1:28,

> God blessed them [ie. man as male and female] and said to them, "Be fruitful and increase in number; fill the earth and subdue it. Rule over the fish of the sea and the birds of the air and over every living creature that moves on the ground."

True, the Hebrew words which are translated here as "subdue", "rule" and "dominion" (in some versions) are used elsewhere in the Old Testament of kings coercing nations into servitude, and of treading grapes. But the forceful language of these verses must be read as part of the whole creation narrative and not wrenched out of context.

Unfortunately, some people have been guilty of a misinterpretation of this passage and have thus brought about some confusion as to the Christian position. The first attacks came in the late 1960s when an American environmentalist called Lynn White asserted that the "dominion" language of Genesis had produced a *domination* attitude towards the global environment. His basic argument (and assumption) runs as follows. Christianity teaches that humanity and nature are separate, and that nature only exists to meet human needs. "Salvation" applies only to humanity on a spiritual dimension. Further, most of the prevalent Christian views on the end times suggest that the present earth only serves this present age and will be destroyed while Christians will be beamed up, after the fashion of Star Trek, to heaven. He also identified a link between the spread of the Christian gospel and the decline of animistic and pagan beliefs in independent "spirit beings" in nature. This too, White claimed, has enabled nature more easily to be exploited.

Few people would disagree that the development of technology and the increased exploitation of the earth's resources is due in part to a change in thinking. Most notably, the ideas that humanity could see itself as distinct from, could control and could dominate nature have been important. These have resulted in a profound and long-lasting change in humanity's relationship to the rest of the natural world over the last few centuries. What is highly debatable is the extent to which Christian beliefs have enabled this sea change.

It is true that industrialisation first emerged in countries where Christianity had a strong influence. Indeed, a relationship with a creative God motivated many thinkers and scientists such as Francis Bacon and Isaac Newton to seek to understand the natural world. As far as opposing paganism is concerned, Christianity has always tried to stand against notions that nature is divine, whilst seeking neither to devalue it nor to encourage its abuse and exploitation. In this tension, no doubt mistakes have been made.

However, it is very easy to overstate the impact of Christianity on the development of the Western industrial culture. Tim Cooper, in his fine book, *Green Christianity*, states that a greater influence has been from the Enlightenment ". . . which elevated human reason as the arbiter of truth and only accepted Christianity in so far as it could be proved by reasoned argument." [31]

It was this so-called "Age of Reason" in the seventeenth and eighteenth centuries that contributed to dualistic thought, which sees spiritual and material elements as completely separate. It was the deist[32] philosopher, Rene Descartes who reduced all reality to what could be understood by the mind: "I think, therefore, I am." In claiming that only rational beings have a soul, he saw no purpose or spiritual life in matter, comparing it to machinery. To him, animals were like clocks and even the human body was mechanical. Descartes and other "enlightened thinkers" have hurried the *decline* of Christian influence in our culture[33] which has gradually been overtaken by secular humanism – the belief that humanity is independent of a creator and is basically good.

Of course it is very difficult to sort out causes and effects in the complexities of human society as it progresses – and regresses – over the centuries. It would seem that some environmentally-aware people have taken a quick look at the present church, and found it largely silent and inactive on green issues. They have then taken a quick look at Genesis and a quick look at the spread of industrialisation and have drawn some rather hasty conclusions. It is quite convenient to have someone or something to blame when you have an ecological crisis on your hands.

Yes, Christianity has contributed to part of the character and some of the attitudes of Western culture. Yes, many of the most prominent inventors and discoverers were sincere Christians. But surely no one is saying that Western industrial culture could properly be described as "Christian". As one green Christian has said, "our problem lies in the Church's historical captivity to Western culture, rather than the reverse" [34]

At the end of the day, the question which is most relevant for our generation is not, "has Christianity got us in this mess?", but rather, "can Christianity show us the way out?". In the chapters that follow, I will be arguing that it is the Christian message which offers most hope and most motivation as a force for change.

Dominion not Destruction

Returning to a more positive view of Genesis 1, the dominion idea can be explained in a number of ways. For a start, a right understanding of God's on-going relationship with the earth he caringly made must exclude any idea of him commanding its ruthless exploitation by humankind. Instead, as God took the earth when it was "formless and empty, and darkness was over the face of the deep" [35] and made something beautiful and full of his goodness, so man has been given the earth, at a later stage, to develop it and harness its potential.

To Boldly Go

Research, invention and discovery were (probably) all in the Lord's mind when he commanded that the earth be filled and subdued. The idea of "subduing" needs to be thought right through. When grapes are trodden, they are not completely destroyed, but exposed to human creativity to make wine. Fields of wheat require many stages to become crusty bread, deep-pan pizzas and sticky buns. Surely, God did not intend that diamonds should be placed deep inside the earth solely for the pleasure of worms!

It is not that nature and natural forces are bad and need to be crushed into submission like an enemy. Neither does all of nature need humanity to complete it. (For God, the pleasure of a frolicking dolphin, an alpine snowscape and an electric storm cannot be bettered). But, within the goodness of creation, people are able to enhance it and to bring a further sense of wholeness to it.

Likewise, we cannot deny that the message of the Bible does contain a sense of progress, development and unfolding revelation. This has been attacked as "linear thinking" by those whose view of the world only accepts reality as a never-ending cycle. The existence of time, history and increasing knowledge would seem to suggest that God intended a sense of advancement. How can new understandings or discoveries be unlearned or, of themselves, represent anything other than progress? One biblical example is the fact that Genesis begins in a garden and Revelation ends in a city.

Of course, the question of how research, technology and inventions are used is a different matter entirely. A classic example of the complexities involved is found in Marie Curie's work. Her discovery of radium at the turn of the century was, and is, a major boon in combating cancer. Yet the information gained from her work on radium has been developed to create nuclear weapons. What irony!

God's Governor

Another view of dominion is based around the idea that people, made in the image of God, are his representatives in the earth. The presence of humanity in the earth is closely related to God's relationship with the world. As the commentator, von Rad has noted, "Just as powerful earthly kings, to indicate their claim to dominion, erect an image of themselves in the provinces of their empire where they do not personally appear, so man is placed on earth as God's sovereign emblem. He is really only God's representative, summoned to maintain and enforce God's claim to dominion over the earth".[36]

This means that humankind cannot simply run riot in the world, like some delinquent England football supporter in Europe. We remain accountable to our sovereign, and will ultimately be asked how we have represented that sovereign. I will return to this thought.

God's Kingdom

A more dynamic vision of Genesis 1:28 does not see humanity in the image of God simply maintaining God's rule, but rather *extending* that rule. Taking each phrase of the verse separately:

Be fruitful and increase in number – not only is this the first biblical command to sexual reproduction, but it also gives the first suggestion of the Kingdom growth principle taught at length by Jesus.[37] However we interpret Genesis 1–3, it is hard to escape the thought that human origins began in a restricted geographical location. Much secular anthropology would endorse this view.

Fill the earth and subdue it – this extension of God's rule must completely cover the earth. Any resistance to his Kingdom must be overcome. Again, I see that this would hardly refer to overcoming nature, which God has called "good", but may include harnessing its power. The overcoming aspect may partly relate to the demonic spiritual forces which attempt to (and, of course, did manage to) usurp God's authority in the earth.

There are two interesting mirror passages to this in the New Testament. The first is Matthew 28: 18,19: "All authority in heaven and on earth has been given to me. Therefore go and make disciples of all nations . . ." I read this to mean that after the tragic event of the Fall,[38] and the passage of thousands of years, Jesus came to restore to humanity the possibility of fulfilling the "cultural mandate" of Genesis 1:28 – that is, to reach *all* humanity, and then *all* creation with the good news of the Kingdom of God.

The second is Revelation 2 and 3. In these chapters, the prophecies given to the seven churches each contain the command to "overcome". The role of the Church, as the primary agency of God's kingdom, is to continue the "subduing" activities of the original cultural mandate. It is wonderful to know that when God has a good idea, he does not throw it in the bin at the first obstacle! Those who have owned the rule of God for their own lives are therefore still involved in this first command.

Rule over the fish of the sea and the birds of the air and over every living creature that moves on the ground – this draws us back into the heart of the question of animals. I will return to the subject again to consider more practical aspects of the treatment of animals later,[39] but it is this phrase which leads us to yet another biblical explanation of the key relationship between humankind and the rest of our environment.

Stewardship

I believe that it is impossible to understand the mandate of Genesis 1:28 apart from its complementary passage in Genesis 2:15,

> "The Lord God took the man and put him in the Garden of Eden to work it and take care of it".

Again the Hebrew words add more depth to this passage than the English implies. The words translated as "take care" are used elsewhere in the Old Testament of serving. Assuming that the Garden of Eden can be taken as a poetic metaphor for the whole earth, this puts some shade on the first commandment. For humankind's destiny is far broader than just to march onwards ruling and subduing as we go. The creative idea of "work" as something constructive, and of our role as caretakers, must always be borne in mind when we think of dominion. It's as if Genesis 1:28 concentrates on our distinctive role within nature, whilst Genesis 2:15 suggests more of our identity *as part of* nature. Again, this does not necessarily mean equality with the rest of nature, but certainly it carries more than a suggestion of partnership.

We must not diminish the created role of humanity, but we must not overstate it. One of the most helpful ways of showing our relationship to animals is to use the distinction between a monarchy and a hierarchy. In a hierarchy, one can identify a clear rank order – the highest in order is clearly a superior; the lowest, an inferior. In a true monarchy, the monarch is a "first among equals". For example, the Queen of England is as human, fallible and as mortal as any of us, but her *role* is superior – *inherently as a person*, she is not.

Quite clearly the most important key in all this is the relationship between people and God. As one reads on in Genesis 2, God sets Adam on his way with this caretaking role by presenting the animals to be named. The naming is very significant because man has played a small, but concluding part in the creation story. The Lord initiated this so that, from the outset, there would be a sense of *responsibility* which people felt towards animals. This responsibility (which does not explicitly preclude all *use* of animals) would be marked out by a clear understanding of *whose* animals they were. This is where the answer lies – the steward never takes on ownership of the property for which he is caring, but must give an account for it.

On a broader level, this idea of stewardship is of profound importance as we seek to work out how to live in this world. In recognising that the earth is the Lord's and everything in it, and that all things were made by God and for him, it should helpfully affect the way in which we treat everything. Materialism becomes an irrelevance. What good is amassing finances, luxury goods or other achievements if they don't truly belong to us anyway? In Luke 12:48 Jesus states that those who have been given much will be demanded to show how they have used their abundance. My house may have my name on the deeds, but God is not too bothered about that – he knows it's only on loan to me! The important question is, do I treat it that way?

Perhaps it is this one truth which is of single-most importance as we allow the bible to speak to our present crisis. Would we dare pollute the air, ravage the forests, torture animals for our table or kill them for our sport if we understood fully that they were not ours to carelessly maim and destroy in the first place?

We should recover the wonder of the psalmist as we consider our role in creation,

"You made [man] ruler over the works of your hands;
you put everything under his feet:
all flocks and herds, and the beasts of the field, the birds of the air,
and the fish of the sea . . .

"O LORD, our Lord,
how majestic is your name in all the earth!" [40]

Notice that the emphasis in the first of these verses – which clearly set out what I have described as the "monarchy principle" - is all on "you" (ie the Lord). It is "you" who made man, and the works of "your" hands over which "you" have placed him.

Finally, Jesus himself teaches accountability through stewardship. There are many pictures of this accountability in his parables – sorting the sheep from the goats; calling his servants to show how they spent their talents; the vineyard owner looking to collect his rent. As we finish this look at stewardship of creation, at the beginning, the Bible takes us to the Last Day. If we must give account for every idle word spoken[41] how much more for every extinct species? As we grasp what it means to be stewards in the image of God, we recognise that the stakes are higher than can ever be imagined.

Summary

In the beginning God gave the earth to humanity as a wonderful present. The response of a grateful people should have been to enjoy it, to fulfil its potential and to actively care for it. Indeed, it should have been presented back to

God in this fulfilled state as a token of our love for him. Instead, global history has taken a very different course, and that potential has not been fulfilled.

The key to the delicate balance of ecology that the Lord God created lay in one pivotal relationship – that between God himself and his steward, Adam. The vision of a harmonious creation, of fulfilled potential in all the earth lay in the hands of humankind. In the next chapter, I want to consider why this relationship was spoiled and what it has meant for the earth.

Notes

1 The origins of this familiar word are in the Greek language. *Biblos* simply means "the book".
2 Exodus 3:14
3 Matthew 6:9
4 See section on "Apologetics" in Appendix 2.
5 Cf. Luke 13:34
6 Colossians 1:16b,17
7 Genesis 1:31
8 This word, not found in the Bible itself, has been used for centuries to describe the fact that whilst God is one, he is actually three persons.
9 Genesis 1:2
10 See John 1:1–3
11 Psalm 24:1
12 Matthew 10:29
13 Matthew 6:29,30
14 Matthew 10:26
15 Verse 5
16 Psalm 104:1,35
17 Theologians call this "sovereign creation *ex nihilo*".
18 This is the main thrust of the philosophical idea known as existentialism.
19 Eg Romans 1:20
20 Put simply, this considers that everything is one and that everything is divine. See also Appendix 1.
21 Hebrews 1:3
22 Romans 8:38,39
23 John 1:3
24 Genesis 1:26,27
25 Genesis 2:7
26 Mark 14:32–40

27 James 2:23
28 Genesis 2:5
29 N Butterworth and I Inkpen, *Wonderful Earth!* Hunt and Thorpe, 1990
30 Genesis 1:31
31 Tim Cooper, *Green Christianity* Spire, 1990, p35
32 See *Deism* in Appendix 2
33 This process is known as "secularisation".
34 Wesley Granberg-Michaelson, quoted in Cooper, *ibid.*
35 Genesis 1:2
36 Quoted in Ferguson and Wright, *New Dictionary of Theology*, p593
37 Eg the parables of the mustard seed (Matthew 13:31,32) and of the yeast (Matthew 13:33).
38 See next chapter.
39 See Chapter 8.
40 Psalm 8:6–9
41 Matthew 12:36

Chapter 4

PARADISE LOST

Fallen Humanity and Nature

The Incredible Price of Freewill
Having painted such a picture of creation – of its splendour and of its purpose – one might be forgiven for a puzzled scratch of the head as one looks at the status quo. If God is so powerful, and yet good and faithful, how in heaven's name could he have allowed this mess to come about?

The answer lies, as I have already indicated, in the key relationship which the Lord built into the equation. To use the language of the parables, it is that between the owner of the vineyard and his tenant – that is, humanity's relations to God.

One of the most essential ingredients in the complex make up of humanity is our inherent ability to choose. Without freewill a whole continent of life and experience is excluded. What is love unless it is given freely? How can we be generous unless we can be mean as well?

Likewise, the principle of stewardship teaches that we have a choice about what we do – not only with our money and with the earth's resources, but also with our emotions. Does someone *make* me angry or do I *choose* to be angry? After six years of marriage am I "in love" (which can sound like a bit of an accident!) or do I choose to love Charlotte? Friendship is the same. My friends are not those to whom I am forced to relate and with whom I share my life, but those whom I deliberately trust, speak to and make contact with.

In the last chapter, we saw that there was a unique

intimacy between God and the people he had created – God desired to have the friendship and companionship of Adam and Eve. But, like the human relationships which mirror that great intended friendship, it was neither compulsory nor robotic.

To enable this freewill really to exist, God had to build a high risk factor into his created world.[1] God placed a large number of choices (or "trees") in the Garden which Adam and Eve were free to make and which would determine their future. However, there was one choice which was non-negotiable. In the poetic language of Genesis 2, this choice – and God's risk – is represented by two trees:

> "In the middle of the garden, were the tree of life and the tree of knowledge of good and evil." [2]

Adam, the depiction of early humanity,[3] was told that he was free to eat of any tree, except the tree of knowledge.[4] The fruit of this tree speaks of more than a juicy and irresistible Cox's orange pippin, as implied by the Renaissance painters.

Instead, the choice which God placed in the middle of the Garden was connected to how Adam was going to relate to God. In the Genesis account there is no further reference to the tree of life, except after the fall when Adam and Eve are told that they are no longer permitted to eat of this tree.[5] Perhaps the choice between the two trees was as simple as that between *life* and *knowledge*. "Life" is more than just existence, but is the essence of being – everlasting life from God himself; lived in fullness and lived in harmony with him. "Knowledge" suggests competing with God – trying to rise to his level and fulfil God-given potential without God's help. As the saying goes, "knowledge is power".

What is most clear is that the significance of Adam's disobedience is deeper than just the accidental breaking of a whimsical command. To use an inadequate illustration, the relationship can be compared to a marriage –

partnerships differ in their character, but the marriages that work are rarely those where partners are competing and seeking to outdo one another – these couples will usually be ripped apart in no time. But where there is a yielding and a humble attitude, there is more chance the marriage will work – not problem-free, but with a commitment to move forward together.

The link between parents and children presents a different model to illustrate the same thing. The parent (or guardian) is clearly in an authority role, the other under authority. This is not a problem whilst it is understood that authority, when not abused, is for us and not against us. The parallel with Adam might be of a 7 year old who is over-confident and thinks he no longer needs a guiding, directing parent.

Before Adam "fell from grace", as his disobedience is commonly described, it is important to understand that he was not in a state of perfection. According to the dictionary, "perfect" means "something done thoroughly or completely; completed; mature; complete." [6] Similarly, one of the Greek words which is used in the New Testament is *teleios*, which signifies "having reached an end, finished, complete, perfect".[7] The over riding thought in the word is one of completeness and wholeness. It is a positive idea, rather than a negative one. For many of us, the idea of perfection is the latter, the *absence* of anything bad or wrong. In fact, perfection requires something more than just a lack of fault.

In its original created form, humankind was like everything else that God had made: full of potential goodness and life, waiting to be fulfilled. If Adam had actually eaten of the other tree, the tree of life, then it is possible that he would have made the choice to develop that potential by the grace of God, and in fellowship and friendship with God. He would then have taken a willing step to fulfil the commandment of Genesis 1:28. By eating of the tree of knowledge, he "fell" and ". . . sin entered the world through one man, and death through sin . . ." [8] His life became tainted by this sin, which is moral evil,[9] and a new law entered the earth – the law of sin and death.[10] It is this law which still rules the human race today, and indirectly rules all creation.

There is not adequate space here to examine the story of the fall in detail, as it is told in Genesis 3. Its many fascinating questions deserve a book in themselves![11] For our purposes, as we look for the root of the ecological crisis, it is enough to say that man and woman used their free-will to disobey God; they ate the "forbidden fruit" and deliberately chose a destiny which denied a humble dependence upon God. The harmony and order which God had intended was (temporarily) lost – the monarch amongst creatures was no longer ruling on behalf of the Creator and this had profound consequences. Satan, represented as the serpent in the narrative,[12] had an important part to play in the whole drama, and was judged by God on account of his deception. Nonetheless, God holds man and woman responsible for their choice – their sin.

Well in advance, God had clearly laid out before Adam what the upshot of his rebellion would be:

> ". . . you must not eat from the tree of the knowledge of good and evil, for when you eat of it you will surely die." [13]

So Adam suffered death from the moment of that separation from God. Of course, he did not immediately die *physically*. Rather, he instantly experienced a *spiritual* death which permanently separated him from his Maker and his God. The Hebrew tense literally renders the passage, "dying, you will die." The death has a direct dimension, as well as one which is delayed. A high price to pay for the knowledge he gained – to quote another saying, "a little knowledge is a dangerous thing"!

Redressing the Balance

All in all, a gloomy state of affairs and no error! Before going on, it is important to say that the fall is not all it's sometimes cracked up to be. Before stoning this book for heresy, let me explain. Given much of the evangelical preaching that one hears, one could be forgiven for thinking that the fall is *the* major event of world history. This can lead people to consider the Fall as more important than the creation in explaining the world's beginnings.

Many Christians are beginning to see that for too long liberals have majored on Genesis 1 and 2 at the expense of Genesis 3, while evangelicals have majored on Genesis 3 at the expense of Genesis 1 and 2. What the Bible presents, however, is the reality of sin in an otherwise good and beautiful creation. It is by no means a totally pessimistic picture.

Whilst the Lord grieves and suffers more than any of us with his suffering creation (particular his human creation[14]), we must not lose sight of the big picture. God made a good earth, Satan tried to ruin it by manipulating the pride and independence of humanity, but God has not let go of it. He has put into effect a plan to rescue the earth and everything in it through his wonderful Son, Jesus. In short, on the plan of eternity, the fall appears in true perspective – a catastrophe for all creation, but only a part of the story.

Broken Image

Before getting on to look at how all this has directly affected our non-human environment, it is essential to note some of the other ways in which Adam's sin has affected the world.

1. Presence of Evil

One of the eternal questions that so puzzles the finite human mind is that of suffering and the presence of evil in the earth. If we believe that when God completed his creative work, looked at its wholeness and described it as "very good", then there is surely no room for evil in our idea of what the original Garden looked like. A God of pure goodness and righteousness cannot create evil. Other religions either proclaim a god who is not all-good, or a god who is not all-powerful. Some theological arguments based in Christianity also try to "get round" the problem.[15] But a truly biblical position must reconcile the presence of evil with a God who is both all-powerful and all-good. We know that evil has been around in the earth since the fall – but where has it come from?

I have already shown that without the ability to choose neither good nor evil could be chosen. Put very simply, this means that free-will is not itself evil, but it is the cause of evil. The nature of evil has been described as being not some*thing*, but the lack of something (ie the *lack* of goodness).

For example, if I wanted to build some shelves and bought some wood (not tropical hardwood, of course!), I would expect it to be perfect. However, if I discovered that the wood had a hole in it, I would think it imperfect. What is wrong with the hole? After all, it's only an innocent mixture of gases: water vapour, oxygen, carbon dioxide, and so on, lurking between some chunks of Spruce, isn't it? The problem is not *what* the hole is, but rather the absence of wood *where* the hole is.

Indeed, some people have described evil as the descent to nothingness. This descent morally can be traced through the early chapters of Genesis, reaching its climax in the judgement of the Flood in chapter 6. If Satan is the adversary of God, he will want to destroy all God has made. He is not merely on the side of evil, promoting it and inciting it; he is evil personified.

Therefore, evil has been brought into being by humankind's abuse of its freewill. "Whereas God created the *fact* of freedom, man performs the *acts* of freedom. God made evil possible; creatures make it actual" [16]

2. Adam versus God

As God is a perfect, righteous and holy God he *cannot* tolerate evil (and sin is evil). It gave him no pleasure to expel Adam and Eve from the Garden[17] – the home he had lovingly made for them. Neither does it please him that the result of sin means that a barrier exists between God and the people he loves today. The Bible reinforces this fact in the New Testament – "The Lord . . . is patient with you, *not wanting anyone to perish*, but *everyone* to come to repentance."[18] (My italics).

This sin-barrier is like a thick cloud obscuring the sun. We know that the sun is still there on a cloudy day, but we cannot see it, feel it, or benefit from its qualities. This is why God promised, even at the moment when he banished Adam and Eve, that the serpent would be crushed[19] and so, implicitly, that the sin-barrier would be removed.

3. Sin spreads

It is not exactly clear how the sin of Adam has affected the entire human race, but the fact that it has is clear both from the rest of the Bible and from observation. The traditional explanation for the spread of the fall's effects is described as "original sin". This says that as Adam had all of humanity in him when he fell, (ie in his genes) everybody is born as a sinner and inevitably sins.

Others suggest that the fall has created a corrupted moral environment in the world. This in turn has made it harder for humanity to resist Satan's temptations. Further, a spiritual blindness has descended upon people: "the god of this age [that is, Satan] has blinded the minds of unbelievers . . ." [20] The human will has somehow been impaired so that we can no longer naturally discern spiritual things.[21]

However we understand it, the outcome is quite clear: "If we claim to be without sin, we deceive ourselves and the truth is not in us."[22] Few of us, even in our most self-righteous moments, would deny that this has more than a ring of truth!

4. Man versus woman

Having already seen how sin has separated humankind from its Creator, we now come on to examine the ways in which the fall has caused rifts *within* the creation. The most immediate way in which this fracture was felt was between the genders. God's curse on the woman included a statement about her bond with man:

> "Your desire will be for your husband, and he will rule over you."[23]

This set in pattern the broken compatibility which is often described in short-hand as the "battle of the sexes". Woman was intended to rule in partnership *with* man – instead she is ruled *by* man. The shame and horrors of sexual degradation, of sexism, of demeaning humour, and of abuse against women are rooted in this calamitous event. As the decline of human morality is traced throughout the Old Testament, it is no wonder that some casual readers have observed that the Bible is full of sex and violence! Sadly, the sex is often an exploitation of women, and they are frequently the victims of violence as well.[24]

5. Man versus man

The fissures within humanity were not only a matter of gender. Unable to fellowship with God, people became insecure. This insecurity led to fear, and fear in turn led to violence. Hatred, anger, envy and greed all stepped into this vacuum. It was only a matter of time before murder ensued – the first account of murder is the well-known story of Cain and Abel. It contains that ultimate rebuff of the integrity of the human race; a denial of man's responsibility before God, "Am I my brother's keeper?"[25]

From murder it is only a few steps to torture, war and genocide. Even on a less dramatic scale, the signs of the rift are everywhere. Racism is a good example. The Lausanne Covenant makes an interesting statement about culture,

> "Because man is God's creature, some of his culture is rich in beauty and goodness. Because he is fallen, all of it is tainted with sin and some of it is demonic."[26]

Much of the sin in culture creates not diversity, but conflict and racial tension. Another example is the partisan spirit. This, the Apostle Paul describes as what it means to be "worldly". When addressing the church in Corinth he says, ". . . since there is jealousy and quarrelling among you, are you not worldly?"[27] Given that humankind cannot get its act together, it is hardly surprising that we have wreaked such havoc in the rest of creation!

6. Image of God versus Image of Sin
One of the most tragic results of the fall, apart from humanity's separation from God, all the grief that sin and evil have caused, and the damage we do to one another, is that the image of God has been broken. The wealth, care and passion which he poured into forming us into something "fearfully and wonderfully made"[28] – something which truly reflected him – has been shamefully tainted. Humour (what an incredibly valuable thing!) became perverted and barbed; sexuality confused and driven by lust; strength became misused to oppress and bully. The goodness is still there somewhere, but so often heavily veiled.

Humankind still bears the image of God, and that is the lesson of creation. Even in the most immoral and evil of people there is usually a flicker of something which reminds one of the Lord himself – gentleness, generosity, or a charming smile. Our unique fingerprints bear witness of the importance of the individual before God. But we also bear another image – the image of sin, pride and rebellion against our Maker and against his plan for us and for our world.

7. Creator versus all creatures
As far as some of these issues are concerned, you might be wondering what sexism, racism and the rest have to do with the environment. My reply to this would be that developing a greener gospel means developing one which is truly wholistic. It will be a gospel which does not separate the issues that endanger the rainforest, that cause pollution, and

that threaten oppressed minorities. God's love will reach the city-dwellers and the ozone-layer. If sin is the true root of all evil, and this sin has touched all the earth, then surely our gospel must move towards seeing that Jesus' work of redemption has also touched all things.

Cursed is the Ground?

The final question to consider as we look at Genesis 3 is one which returns us to the heart of developing an "eco-sound" theology: how did the fall affect the non-human creation?

At this point it is worth setting out in full Genesis 3:17b–19. These verses provide the crucial link between the spiritual crisis described in the last section, and the ecological crisis (which is, in fact, just as spiritual in itself) which remains the focus of this book.

> To Adam [God] said, . . .
> "Cursed is the ground because of you;
> through painful toil you will eat of it
> all the days of your life.
> It will produce thorns and thistles for you,
> and you will eat the plants of the field.
> By the sweat of your brow
> you will eat your food
> until you return to the ground,
> since from it you were taken;
> for dust you are
> and to dust you will return."

First, let's remind ourselves that it was Adam and Eve who sinned. As the monarchs of creation, and the only creatures made in God's image, they alone *could* sin. Any consequences of the fall which are felt other than by humanity, must directly relate to the sin of the first Mr and Mrs.

Second, we must try to make the connection between the goodness of creation, the catastrophe of sin and what we see in the world today. Without setting aside the complexity of this question, I want to consider three dimensions of the status quo.

1. A world full of beauty, majesty and relationship

There is still a great deal in the world to inspire our hearts and minds and to draw our wonder and praise. When I was a new Christian believer I was taught that the fall had spoiled *everything* God had made. Because sin has touched everything – the landscapes, the animals and birds – it was all warped in some way. So warped in fact that God was going to burn it up whilst we went off to heaven. I used to be baffled by the thought that even the most breath-taking sunset over Pagham Harbour was no better than a "quality second" as far as the Lord was concerned.

What a great relief and a great revelation, when I discovered that the power of sin is not so great as to obliterate God's fingerprints entirely from the natural world. No, much of what we now see in the creation is still as God intended it to be.

2. Humanity's direct impact

The second ingredient in what we now see in the world is several thousand years of the (mis)management of the earth by *homo sapiens*. I showed earlier that because people have been put out of relationship with God, we cannot relate properly to our brothers or sisters. It is the same lack of relationship which is at the root of so much of the environmental grief which we are currently experiencing. Without relationship to God, notions of stewardship and dominion make no sense, and are therefore not practised.

Our failure to care properly for the earth has caused the creation to bleed. Across every culture – regardless of religion or philosophy – greed and selfishness have meant that we humans abuse our rights of dominion. Because this selfishness and greed for personal gain have become such a strong motivation, we even seem willing to jeopardise the well-being of future generations. Of course, sustaining the earth for our children is a relatively selfish motive compared to how we should be stewarding the earth – treating it as a wonderful present of which the Lord has kindly let us take care.

Behind all the human-made problems of the environment lies this one great cause. In the place of the one true God, people worship idols, which includes science, technology and material prosperity. In the West, these have served to add fuel to the ecological flames.

3. Suffering in the Creation

It is quite simple to look at the positive qualities in the earth and state unhesitantly that they are God's handiwork. It is equally straightforward to blame humanity for the destructive abuse of our environment. As far as the so-called "darker side" of nature is concerned, it becomes less simple. Indeed, it is very difficult to be precise about what creation was like before the fall.

Perhaps we should see a link between the darker side of nature and the darker side of humanity. People are capable of wonderful acts of beauty, love and generosity, but also of meanness, jealousy and hideous acts of cruelty. A friend of mine once commented how aware he is of his own mixed motives. Even in his love for his wife, there is the selfish pleasure he receives from their relationship; even in worshipping God, a hint of pride and self-satisfaction. This mixture is reflected in nature.

For example, when I was young we had a family pet: Whiskey the marmalade cat. He was born at the bottom of our garden and was soon abandoned by his mother. This made him dependant upon our saucers of milk, and eventually our tins of "Go-cat". As he grew up we became very fond of him and his amusing, unique character. Then we moved to a new house which backed onto some riding stables. For the first few weeks he daily brought back two or three mice which, with precise cruelty, he played with and teased until they died. To us, a much-loved pet; to the mouse community of Belfairs Park, a terminator of truly horrifying proportions!

The paradox is that we cannot really separate the bits of nature which we like from those which we do not. Gorse bushes can be agonising to walk through, but where would the rare smooth snake and the charismatic Dartford warbler nest without them? Perhaps the New Testament can aid us here. Paul used language in Romans 8 which indicates something of this tension,

> "The creation waits in eager expectation for the sons of God to be revealed. For the creation was subjected to frustration, not by its own choice, but by the will of the one who subjected it, in hope that the creation itself will be liberated from its bondage to decay and brought into the glorious freedom of the children of God. We know that the whole creation has been groaning as in the pains of childbirth right up to the present time. Not only so, but we ourselves, who have the firstfruits of the Spirit, groan inwardly as we wait eagerly for our adoption as sons, the redemption of our bodies."[29]

I will return to look at this passage in more detail in the next chapter, but for now we can gain some valuable insights from some of the words used.

The word translated as "frustration" is *mataiotes* which means an emptiness, or failure of the results designed. If all God made was essentially good, this failure must have been caused by sin (that is, creation was subjected to frustration by Adam). The use of *mataiotes* underlines the idea that within creation there was potential – either to be released through humanity into eternity, or to be held through human sin in bondage.

"Decay" is even more clearly a negative concept. This is the Greek word *phthora* (pronounce that!) which signifies corruption, destruction or being made inferior. The language again leads us towards the thought of sin impacting the neutrality of an unfulfilled creation. Further, I have described evil as a lapsing towards nothing. This also seems parallel to a rule of decay.

4. Summary

One of the most compelling thoughts which comes through Paul's sketch of a creation waiting to be rescued and redeemed, is that it is linked with a rescued and redeemed humanity. It is hard to see that this could be so without the rule of decay in creation being linked with the law of sin and death in humanity.

Man and woman are the creatures whom God has placed at the pinnacle of his creation to rule as first amongst equals. Within the order of the natural world, people could rule properly only whilst in humble fellowship and friendship with God. When Adam and Eve rebelled against God, that set in motion something physical whereby the earth rebelled against man, typified by thorns and thistles. The whole world has been thrown "out of synch." Hence creation is groaning awaiting a release.

God decided sovereignly to provide this release – this salvation. He purposed to heal all the fractures and allow all the potential to be fulfilled. He never abandoned his plan for the whole creation. But his image, humankind, was to remain the key.

Notes

1 Some Christians hold the view that God is completely outside time and therefore knows everything about the future. This would mean that in creating the possibility of evil, he knew that Adam would choose disobedience and therefore bring evil into being. Whilst the Bible is not conclusive on this matter, some have pointed out that this interpretation presents a bit of a moral problem. The alternative argument would go on to suggest that in creating a world which is in time and space, it can be inferred that God's existence and dealings are also somehow sequential.

2 v.9.
3 Adam is Hebrew for "man".
4 Vs. 16,17.
5 Genesis 3:22.
6 Chambers 1981, p.989.
7 WE Vine *A Comprehensive Dictionary of the Original Greek words with their Precise Meanings for English Readers* p.855.
8 Romans 5:12.
9 Again, New Testament Greek can help us to understand this word. The Bible word translated as "sin" in English, is usually the word, *hamartia*, which originates in archery, "to miss the mark". Thus, even the idea of sin means a failure to fulfil potential.
10 See Romans 8:12 and 5:12–21.
11 I recommend JE Colwell's article in *The New Dictionary of Theology* (IVP, 1988) as a fairly painless place to start.
12 Briefly, Satan is the enemy and adversary of God, and so of God's image, humankind. He is an angel, and therefore another of God's creatures. Like Adam and Eve though, he chose to try to equal God and was cast from heaven.
13 Genesis 2:17.
14 See Matthew 10:29–31.
15 Eg Panentheism claims that suffering is part of God's continuing process of creation.
16 See *Evil* in the *New Dictionary of Theology Ibid.*, p.242.
17 See Genesis 3:23.
18 2 Peter 3:9.
19 See Genesis 3:15.
20 2 Corinthians 4:4.
21 See 1 Corinthians 2:14.
22 1 John 1:8.
23 Genesis 3:16b.
24 The attitude of Lot to his daughters' virginity in Genesis 19 and the particularly gruesome story of Judges 19 are but two of many examples.
25 Genesis 4:9.
26 Para 10, "Evangelism and Culture", quoted in J Stott *Issues Facing Christians Today* Marshalls 1984 p.207.
27 1 Corinthians 3:3.
28 See Psalm 139:13–16.
29 Romans 8:19–23.

Chapter 5

PARADISE REGAINED

Nature Restored and Fulfilled

Every Lost Sheep

There is a story of a shepherd in Palestine many years ago. He was not considered to be a particularly bright, talented or capable man. If he had possessed any of these qualities it is unlikely he would have been a shepherd – the socially unacceptable occupation of the day. But this shepherd was good at his job. Like all shepherds in Palestine, he led his sheep from the front, rather than driving them from behind, as in the West. What's more, he knew his sheep individually and was alert to the dangers they may face.

One day, whilst in the hills, he noticed that one of the sheep was missing. He had already travelled a long distance that day, and the sheep could have strayed anywhere. What should he do? How would he explain the loss to the sheep's owner? His solution was simple and immediate – go after the lost sheep. He was aware of the risk of leaving the rest of the flock in open country, but he was not willing to give up on the one. When eventually he found that sheep, he returned joyfully to his friends in the village and held a party to celebrate the finding of his lost sheep.

No doubt this story caused a few chortles at the expense of the shepherd when told by the Saloon Bar joker at the local tavern. But when it was told by Jesus[1] it took on a different dimension. He used it to show that his heavenly Father was beside himself to save what had been lost. He was willing to take risks and to be imaginative to lift up what had fallen and to restore what had been wasted. He also showed that every individual counts: God does not just see "an ecological crisis", any more than he sees "a large number of people were killed . . .". In each case I believe he sees people, animals, and even geographical areas individually.

At the close of the last chapter we left creation groaning under the effects of humanity's failure to bring it into its intended liberty. We also saw humanity itself groaning and decaying as it served under the ruthless law of sin and death. Like the shepherd, God was not about to write this one off.

Old Testament Milestones

The early biblical landmarks after Genesis 3 are not particularly encouraging – the first murder in Genesis 4 leading downwards to a state of "man's great wickedness" by Genesis 6. So decayed was the situation that we read, in a very moving passage, of God's regrets over the whole business of the human creation.

> "The Lord was grieved that he had made man on the earth, and his heart was filled with pain."[2]

In the following judgement of the flood, every child who has been to Sunday School knows that each species of animal was involved in the rescue plan of Noah's ark. Precise interpretations may differ, but the message is clear – this was not for humanity's sake alone, but to maintain the unity of creation. The whole event provides an early picture of the Lord's intention *completely* to rescue his creation.

After the flood had passed, God made a covenant[3] with Noah. It began with what was basically a repeat of the so-called cultural mandate of Genesis 1:28.[4] It is interesting to note that only after the flood do we read of specific permission for people to eat meat,[5] and further, God said that he would "demand an accounting from every animal."[6] This is illustrated in the law of Moses when every animal that killed a man or woman was also to be killed.[7]

Genesis 11 tells the story of the Tower of Babel (which means "confusion"), and the origins of different languages. It would seem that before this time no one had ventured far beyond what is now known as the Middle East.[8] From our perspective, this introduces yet another breakdown of harmony and wholeness, resulting as it does from human pride and disobedience.

The great event which dominates the rest of the Old Testament is the call of Abraham and the subsequent covenant which God made with him concerning his offspring. In terms of his plan to free the creation from its bondage, God's election of Abraham was a critical step. His idea was to take one righteous man, supernaturally enable him and his (barren) wife to bear a son, and from this son bring a whole nation into being. The nation would be given commandments to show them how to live God's way and so demonstrate the intended rule of God in the earth. The scope of this covenant was far from narrow. Rather, through Abraham, "all peoples on earth will be blessed",[9] and through them the rest of creation.

One Nation under God

Israel was chosen, not *just* to be God's visual aid to the rest of the world, but also to have that friendship with him which the Lord had so missed since Eden. This sentiment is summed up in the oft-repeated phrase, "I will be your God, and you shall be my people".[10] It is quite beyond our comprehension that the Lord - almighty and infinitely holy, who is so far before all things and above all things – should long for this companionship. Yet even Jesus at his darkest hour did not want the comfort of an angel, but desired the company of his friends.

Commandments were entrusted to Moses on Mount Sinai during the period of Israel's exodus from Egypt, and are known collectively as "the Law". The Law was given on the eve of Israel's inheritance of the "promised land" of Canaan,[11] when it was to come fully into force. Its main purpose was two-fold. First, it was intended to indicate the standards of personal, social and environmental morality that God expected of a people who carried his name. More even than morality, the politics, health, ecology and economy of Israel was to show the wisdom and life of God to the nations roundabout.

Second, the Law was intended as a sort of pre-cursor to Christ – showing us that we need a new power of righteousness to be able to live up to this moral standard. This is why Paul says the Law has been "put in charge to lead us to Christ . . .".[12]

As far as our terms of reference are concerned, the Law encapsulates a number of timeless truths about humanity's relationship with the creation. Regarding the build-up of personal wealth, the proper use of land and the treatment of animals, there was plenty of material to guide Israel in developing a right attitude towards the environment. The qualities the Lord plainly required (and equally plainly, still requires) were justice, restraint and compassion.[13]

1. Just distribution of wealth

The land of Israel was to be divided fairly between eleven of the twelve tribes. (The Levites had no specific allotment – their role as priests meant that their inheritance was to be the Lord, and they were given a number of towns in which to live.) Amongst the tribes the land was divided into clans, and amongst the clans into families.[14] It seems that the norm was for each family's land to pass to the next generation. The sale and purchase of land outside the family was very rare (and was generally considered morally wrong[15]), and if circumstances dictated that the sale of some land was unavoidable, provision was made for the land to be "redeemed", or bought back, by a relative.[16]

This appears quite radical in its stability and equality compared to the extremes of poverty and wealth with which we have become familiar. It also demonstrates a high regard for family. But the best is yet to come. Every fifty years, a special Year of Jubilee was to be held. The outstanding feature of this year, when liberty was to be proclaimed, was that all the land which had been sold in the previous forty-nine years was returned to its original ownership. When I first read the Bible I was training to be a conveyancing solicitor – I had to pull up a chair when I got to Leviticus 25!

The whole passage rings with a sense of rightness and justice, containing such commands as:

> "Do not take advantage of each other, but fear your God." (v.17)

> "The land must not be sold permanently, because the land is mine and you are but aliens and my tenants." (v.23)

Naturally, under these circumstances poverty was tempered and hope was not crushed – however grim things seemed, Jubilee was coming! Likewise, the greedy accumulation of land (which was wealth in an agrarian culture) was also tempered.

The tragedy is that there is no evidence that Jubilee was ever practised at all in Israel, and was almost certainly ignored on a national scale. The rest of the Old Testament refers to it more in the breach than in the observance. Like much of church history which was to follow, the values of the world invaded God's community, rather than the reverse.

2. Restrained use of land

A towering example of the fact that God is not just interested in people, but in the wholeness of creation, is also given in other Levitical laws. Every seventh year was to be a Year of Sabbath, reflecting God's rest after the creation, as did the weekly day of Sabbath. On this day no work was to be done by man or animal. In the Sabbath year there was to be no sowing and no pruning of vineyards. The people were allowed to pick whatever grew, but could not directly intervene in the management of the land. God anticipated the fears about what would be eaten in the seventh year, but said, "I will send you such a blessing in the sixth year that the land will yield enough for three years."[17]

After seven Sabbath years, there was to be the Year of Jubilee, tying together justice for humanity and restraint for the land in a great year of peace. The clear suggestion is that if God's commands are obeyed then the rebellion of the earth against humanity, as recorded in Genesis 3, could be partially reversed and the land produce greater fruit in greater wholeness.

Some would no doubt seek to reduce the significance of this passage to the level of sound husbandry in a primitive agrarian society – helpful 3500 years ago but totally inappropriate today. I would strongly contest this argument. Firstly, this is not the only instance where we can see God's care for the land. It would take a highly spiritualised interpretation of Ezekiel 36:8–12 to shed it of all practical implication.

> "But you, O mountains of Israel, will produce branches and fruit for my people Israel, for they will soon come home. I am concerned for you and will look upon you with favour; you will be ploughed and sown, and I will multiply the number of people upon you . . ."[18]

Further, there are a number of other incidental references which encourage a restrained attitude to the land. A nice one is found in Deuteronomy 20:19, where Israel is forbidden from chopping down trees around a beseiged city, "Are the trees of the field people, that you should beseige them?"

Secondly, the statements about the nature of the land, and of its relationship both to God *and* to the people indicate that these passages do contain timeless principles. Naturally, we must do some hard thinking to work out how these apply to our society, but we cannot simply ignore the teaching.

3. Compassionate use of animals

However strongly committed to the rights of animals one

may be, it is impossible to find any support from Scripture for the idea that people should not use animals at all. Having said this, the Law contains a number of references to the proper use of animals. Animals were not to be over-worked or caused discomfort,[19] were not to be denied a share of the benefits of their work,[20] were to be helped out of trouble,[21] and were not to work on the Sabbath day.[22] A summary of this thoughtful approach is provided in Proverbs, "A righteous man cares for the needs of his animal".[23]

As has been said already, the key to this is to understand that the animals do not belong to us, any more than does the soil. The earth is still the Lord's and everything in it, and we must account to him for our use of all created life.

There are two main objections which may be made to this compassionate view of animals in the Old Testament. The first relates to spiritualised interpretations of texts relating to animals. For example, Paul used two of the passages referred to above (ie Deuteronomy 22:10 and 25:4) to draw out spiritual points in his letters. The one is used in connection with relationships between Christian believers and unbelievers, and the other with supporting church-workers financially. Because they are used in a different context in the New Testament, does this mean that their original relevance no longer applies? No, surely it is because the original law was (and is) true and right that it can be applied in a broader way.

The second objection concerns animal sacrifices. Looking back in history from our sensitised context, the number of animals killed under the Old Testament sacrificial system appears quite barbaric. A closer look might bring some qualification to this.

i) It must be remembered that some of the surrounding cultures practised human (child and adult) sacrifice. Tragically, these hideous practices even seeped into the late Kingdom of Israel. By comparison, the Mosaic sacrifices were humane.

ii) The methods of sacrifice (ie draining the lifeblood) actually prevented the cruel practice of ripping individual limbs off live animals which was common elsewhere at that time.

iii) The animals are God's anyway, and how they live and die (which all creatures eventually do!) is surely up to him.

iv) The sacrificial system was only intended as a temporary measure, conveying the idea that no person can enter God's presence because of their sin. As an extension of grace, God allowed the blood of the sacrifice to atone[24] for the sin of the individual. The need for the shedding of blood[25] reveals the horror of sin and foreshadows the coming of Christ. Indeed, the whole sacrificial system ended with perfect self-sacrifice of Jesus, the Lamb of God.

v) God frequently made it clear through his prophets that he did not accept the sacrifices of those whose heart motives were not pure.

This leaves the question of vegetarianism until later.

The Lord – the People – the Land

By looking in at these windows of justice, restraint and compassion, one can see in the Law of Moses something of a restoration of the vision of stewardship and wholeness of Genesis 2:15. However, it adds something as well: a link between the people of Israel and the *land* of Israel which ties in with their relationship to God himself.

Throughout the history of Israel it is impossible to separate the activities and prosperity of God's people from their response to God and their treatment of the land. From the Law onwards through the wisdom literature of Psalms and Proverbs, and right into the Prophets, the Bible constantly refers to "the land" in a very personal way.[26] Some of the language used clearly employs poetic licence, but the message is clear: Israel lacked a sense of completeness when it was not in harmony with the land. This is never more evident than when we read of how the land will respond to Israel's breach of the Covenant:

> Keep all my decrees and laws and follow them, so that the land where I am bringing you to live may not vomit you out.[27]

This all sounds pretty messy! Of course, this is precisely what did occur in the end. After hundreds of years of ignoring these laws, and after dozens of prophets had been martyred for speaking out against the nation's sin, Israel was thrown off the land. Again, if we are tempted to trivialise this dimension by suggesting that the land being active is purely figurative, the exiles to Assyria and Babylon should be remembered.

Exile was the most acutely appropriate of punishments to discipline and teach Israel. When Israel was exiled, they were not Israel. The psalms and laments that speak of the people's weeping and longing for Zion are more than just homesickness.[28] They are about a true loss of identity outside of God-given geography. God was, and still is, passionately interested in geography, and all it contains – animal, mineral and vegetable.

Because the Jewish mind did not think dualistically,[29] the Bible does not separate the sins committed directly *against* the land from those committed *in* the land. Failure to observe the Sabbath years had a direct impact upon the ground itself, but the worship of false gods also "defiled [the] land" and "filled [God's] inheritance with . . . detestable idols."[30] It is interesting to note that, through the prophet, God here invokes the landlord/tenant imagery of stewardship.

This whole issue offers a crucial angle in the story of Israel's failure to fulfil God's covenant. It is also one which is often missed. Unbelief, social injustice and idolatry were all key factors and have been taught at length, but it is this question of "the land" which needs some further exploration.

Messiah

The fact is that Israel failed to fully demonstrate the rule of God and the ways of God. But there was never a time without hope. Even at the moments when God's people seemed furthest from his will – oppressing the poor, moving boundary stones and worshipping false gods – the Lord offered words of great hope. A vision of peace was extended.

> "[The Lord] will judge between the nations
> and will settle disputes for many peoples.
> They will beat their swords into ploughshares
> and their spears into pruning hooks.
> Nation will not take up sword against nation,
> nor will they train for war any more."[31]

There was still hope for salvation to touch everything that God had made.

> "I will also make you a light for the Gentiles,
> that you may bring my salvation to the ends of the earth."[32]

The scarlet thread of joyful hope which runs throughout the prophetic vision of the future was the one who would bring all this about – Messiah!

> "Rejoice greatly, O Daughter of Zion!
> Shout, Daughter of Jerusalem!
> See, your King comes to you,
> righteous and having salvation,
> gentle and riding on a donkey,
> on a colt, the foal of a donkey."[33]

This Messiah was Jesus, God's anointed Son and servant: fully man and yet fully God.[34] He was born of a woman, but was never created. On him rested all the hopes of his people, and of the whole world.

The Life of Christ

If one looks in the Bible to discover how Jesus treated the environment, one finds that direct references are rather few and far between. In fact, most of his comments and actions concerning plants, animals and the earth are either figurative (illustrations or prophetic statements) or incidental.

However, I have already referred to the fact that Jesus clearly demonstrated God's care and interest in nature. In pointing to the sparrows: most common and unlovely among birds, he said that none fall without his Father's knowledge[35] – indeed the Father is described as feeding them personally.[36] In speaking of the lilies, he favourably compared their God-given splendour with the finest of human attire,[37] and the growing seed of corn is a mysterious wonder.[38]

Further, Jesus was very fond of using pictures from the natural world to explain the Kingdom of Heaven.[39] As I suggested in Chapter 3, it would seem that God has deliberately encased many spiritual laws in nature for us to discover. The tiny mustard seed which grows into "the largest of garden plants"[40]; the weeds that cannot be dug up until the harvest is ready[41]; the tender twigs and shoots of the fig tree in Spring[42] – all provide us with clues and insights into the ways of God himself.

Some have actually argued that Jesus has presented a very anthropocentric (or human-centred) view of the world. After all, he was certainly not a vegetarian. He is recorded as eating fish[43] and, as a good Jew, would have eaten lamb at the Passover meal.[44] Additionally, the verse from Matthew 10 referred to above clearly shows that humanity is more valuable to God than other creatures.

An oft-quoted example of Jesus' apparent lack of green credentials is the incident of the deliverance of the Gadarene demoniac found in Mark 5.[45] In this story Jesus is confronted with a man who is possessed by many demons. The demons recognise Jesus for who he really is and plead to be cast out of the man and into a nearby herd of pigs. Jesus complies with this request, after which the pigs run into Lake Galilee and drown. Most commentators are swift to draw something similar to the following conclusion: "The sacrifice of brute and property is justifiable where the sanity and lives of persons are at stake. One man is of more value than many swine."[46]

Whilst there may be some truth in this statement, it hardly gives the full picture. The geographical area where this incident took place was one of the few in rural Palestine which held a mixed population of Jews and Gentiles. The presence of pigs, whose meat was ceremonially unclean for the Jew, was an image of the spiritual impurity and hypocrisy of a large part of first-century Israel. What's more, it was most likely to have been the Jews who benefited commercially from the pig-farming. When the demons were cast into the pigs (at their request), the destruction of the demons was a picture of the impact of God's Kingdom on Satan's kingdom. But the destruction of the pigs was also a picture of Jesus purifying the land.[47]

This episode is but one example of the need to tie a specific passage into the general flow of Scripture, by means of its context.[48] It is particularly important, when reading about Jesus, to remember why the Gospels were written.

Firstly, they were certainly never intended to be pure biography, detailing the historical facts of Jesus' life. Even Luke, the physician, who was known as an historian, skipped from Jesus' first to around his thirtieth year in a few dozen words. We should not expect to find in the Gospels a kind of proof-text way to live: "I'll do what I read Jesus doing and I won't do what I don't read him doing." Taken literally, this would exclude the proper disciple from laughter, riding a bike and going to the loo!

Rather, the accounts of Jesus' life as recorded in the Gospels offer a view of his earthly ministry from the viewpoint of salvation history. Jesus fulfilled all the hope and longing of the Old Testament, and looked forward to the completion of his fruitful work at the end of this age. Following Jesus, the rest of the New Testament is about the Church which he brought into being, and its role of taking Jesus' salvation to all creation. Thus, the Gospels provide an axis in history, not the final chapter of the story.

Secondly, the Gospels are unashamedly people-centred.

As we saw in the last chapter, the frustration and bondage to decay which the creation is suffering are due to humanity's sin and failure. Putting things right between the monarch of creation and the Creator himself was essential to unravelling the whole tangled mess. The apostle Paul describes Jesus as the "last Adam" in 1 Corinthians 15, and in Ephesians 2 he speaks of a new humanity in Christ. It was Jesus Christ who lived the first human life on earth in perfect relationship with the rest of the Godhead. Perfect, that is, until he took all the sin of the world onto himself and died in substitution for each and every one of us. It was his resurrection from death that secured a fresh start for humankind and by which God ". . . reconciled the world to himself in Christ, not counting men's sins against them."[49]

Thirdly, Jesus evidently lived a sustainable life in peace with all that God has made. He modelled a simplicity of lifestyle, not shunning the hospitality of those who were well-off, but owning few possessions himself. He clearly lived a kind of communal life with his friends and followers during the three years of his Messianic ministry, and his message was attractive to those from all tiers of society. However, he spoke out fearlessly against the accumulation of wealth, and frequently sided with the poor. Indeed, there is probably no person who has ever known such poverty – coming from the glory of heaven to live on earth as a suffering servant and to die a naked, criminal's death.[50]

Of course, Jesus did say that he came to bring not peace, but a sword[51] – how does this fit with a message of life and wholeness? Whilst his mission was indeed to bring good news, the cost of following Jesus has always been high and some rejected this message. Further, he had come to declare war on Satan and on the dark forces which held humanity and all creation in bondage. His prediction was thus that in the short-term his ministry would produce division.

I have already said that to describe "green" as something which relates to nothing more than our physical, non-human environment is surely too limited to be of much value. If

green-living is about a wholesome and wholistic life, taking care of what we have been given and bridging divides, then Jesus is certainly an important role-model. He stood against every social barrier he found in his culture:
sexism - consider his dealings with the Samaritan woman,[52] Mary of Bethany[53] and the importance of his other female disciples;[54]
racism - Jesus chose to travel through Samaria and speak to Samaritans (old enemies of the Jews) rather than avoiding the area as was the common practice. When his message was received there he even stayed with the people for two days.[55] He also gladly healed Gentiles and Roman soldiers (the hated occupying army of Israel);[56]
clergy/laity - Jesus saved his fiercest condemnation for "the religious people" who thought themselves more righteous than the rest, but did nothing to help them;[57]
rich/poor - in the story of the rich man and Lazarus,[58] and in conversation with the rich young ruler[59] Jesus again demands that every individual holds a wider responsibility than just for themself;
have/have nots - on the same theme of responsibility and stewardship, we have the example of Jesus' parables.[60] If God has blessed us, then we do have a duty to use what we hold well and share it with others: ". . . Every one to whom much is given, of him much will be required . . ." (RSV)[61].

All this teaching and example on right relationships and wholeness marries in neatly with what we have seen from the Old Testament. At the very outset of his ministry Jesus entered his local synagogue, and at the invitation of the local elders read the following prophecy from Isaiah 61:

The Spirit of the Lord is on me,
because he has anointed me
to preach good news to the poor.
He has sent me to proclaim freedom for the prisoners
and recovery of sight for the blind,
to release the oppressed
to proclaim the year of the Lord's favour.[62]

"The year of the Lord's favour" was a popular phrase to evoke the idea of the Year of Jubilee – of freedom, justice and restored wholeness. It also signified a commitment to fulfil "the Law and the Prophets".[63]

Fourth and finally, we should not assume that the message of Jesus was limited to humankind. That great "gospel in a nutshell" statement of the apostle John says it well enough.

> "For God so loved the world that he gave his one and only Son, that whoever believes in him shall not perish but have eternal life."[64]

The Greek word for "world" is *kosmos*; a term used so frequently in the New Testament that it has at least seven distinct meanings. If one reads John's Gospel from the opinion that Jesus's salvation work was purely people-centred, then "world" will clearly mean no more than the human race.[65]

However, this does not take consideration of the primary meaning of *kosmos* which is order, arrangement, ornament.[66] Given this, John's choice of kosmos is very important. It serves to reinforce the idea that humanity has a place in the "order" of creation which has been so misused to damage that order. Because God so loved the arrangement which he carefully and caringly made in the beginning, he sent Jesus to straighten it out.

Calvary

Given our bird's eye scan across the landscape of salvation history, it is impossible to do proper justice to the central theme of the Cross of Christ. I have already mentioned that his death was one of an innocent substitute, dying in the place of guilty sinners. John 3:16 demonstrates that the result of Jesus's sacrifice was eternal life for all who believed: a complete forgiveness and remission of sin, removing us from the government of sin and death. The power of that sin and death are broken forever.

It is plain that this salvation is quite optional – as Adam

had been given the choice of trees in the garden, so we are given the choice of belonging to the first Adam or to the last Adam. But where does this leave the Christian believer, once the power of sin is broken? Are we back in the same condition as the first Adam, in a state of incomplete sinlessness? Surely we are not. Once the choice is made to follow Christ, and to forsake the lives we have lived apart from God, we enter the new humanity where,

> "There is neither Jew nor Greek, slave nor free, male nor female, for . . . all [are] one in Christ Jesus."[67]

The choice to follow Jesus, I believe, is directly parallel to Adam's opportunity to eat the fruit of the tree of life. Death follows one choice; eternal life the other. Once eternity is introduced into the mix, everything begins to look different, and that is the dynamic force behind church history!

What's more, the curses of the fall were also broken by the one who ". . . [became] a curse for us . . ."[68]. Every point at which Satan had gained a grasp on humanity and on the earth was covered: his power was smashed and the liberating Jubilee had arrived. To use one of the biblical phrases for salvation, God had redeemed, or bought back, humanity from slavery.

But how do we make the connection between where we are now (not yet apparently enjoying the fullness of eternity!) and the fruit of this salvation? Further, how does human salvation affect the rest of the planet? Surely if God wanted to correct the ills of sin and death, he would not simply confine his saving power to humanity. As the writer of the letter to the Hebrews says,

> "In putting everything under him, God left nothing that is not subject to him. Yet at present we do not see everything subject to him".[69]

To answer these questions, we must consider what the

Bible has to say about the end times, or to use the theological term, eschatology.[70]

And in the End

Eschatology is another of those subjects which has exercised the minds of many a Christian over the years. There is obviously a fascination with speculation about the future. On this subject, one thing is certain – you can never quite end an argument until *the* end itself comes!

Just as our present knowledge can help us to understand the past, so our beliefs about the future affect our current outlook. For example, I might promise my son a walk to the beach after lunch, on condition that he does not commit actual bodily harm against his sister in the meantime. I am confident that even my three-year-old is capable of making a choice about his behaviour based upon the future prospects I have set before him! In a similar way, if I believe that this earth will perish in the end times, this belief will also affect my behaviour. I will probably be de-motivated from taking positive environmental action no matter how aware I am that the earth is God's creation.

It is for this reason that the question of eschatology is important. The Christian view of history is distinct in that it rejects the idea of never-ending cycles. God has marked a beginning and an end to world history and he relates with his creation throughout its course. According to Scripture Jesus, who ascended to heaven shortly after his resurrection, will return to earth to raise all the human dead, bring judgement for sin, complete the destruction of Satan and usher in the "age to come". This much is fairly clear although, as I have suggested, there is also much which is vigorously debated.

Ignoring many of the entertaining controversies, the central question as we conclude this chapter remains, "what is the final fate of the earth?" One of the more well-known biblical passages concerning the end of the age is 2 Peter 3:13.

". . . in keeping with his promise we are looking forward to a new heaven and a new earth, and the home of righteousness."

This is mirrored by the vision of John.

"Then I saw a new heaven and a new earth, for the first heaven and the first earth had passed away . . ."[71]

Viewed at first glance, these passages are often taken to mean that the present order will be destroyed and replaced by a new one. This notion is apparently supported by the language of 2 Peter 3:10–12, which speaks of the elements being "destroyed by fire", everything in the earth "burning up", and the elements "melting in the heat". Added to this is the apocalyptic passage in Matthew 24, referring to earthquakes and famines as signs of the end of the age. The overall suggestion is that the earth is so rotten with the sin of the world that it is cracking up. It is beyond hope and beyond redemption – fit only to be discarded.

On the other hand, these verses could be interpreted far more positively. If we consider redemption from humanity outwards, it is quite clear that our present physical bodies will return to dust. (As the saying goes, "death is life's great certainty"!) However, it is equally clear that the Christian's future destiny is not to have a permanent "out of body experience". In 1 Corinthians 15:35ff Paul writes of the "spiritual bodies" which we will receive at the resurrection of the dead. "We will not all sleep, but we will all be changed – in a flash, in the twinkling of an eye . . ."[72] It would seem that we humans are not so rotten with sin that any of us are beyond redemption. So complete was the work of Jesus on the cross that no sin can ever separate the believer from God. As Jesus cried victoriously at the moment of his death, "It is finished!"[73]

If the spiritual change which happens to a Christian believer can result in a physical change, why can the same not be true of the whole creation? If this were so then the "new heavens and the new earth" could well signify a *transformation* rather than a *replacement*. Perhaps the power of God touching the physical elements is just what would have happened if Adam had brought eternity into Eden through the tree of life. I expect to be able to recognise my friends in the age to come; likewise the creation will be recognisable. It will be released from its bondage to decay and will undergo major changes. If not, how ever could Isaiah's prophecy come true?

"The wolf will live with the lamb,
the leopard will lie down with the goat,
the calf and the lion will feed together;
and a little child will lead them.
The cow will feed with the bear,
their young will lie down together,
and the lion will eat straw with the ox.
The infant will play near the hole of the cobra,
and the young child put his hand into the viper's nest.
They will neither harm nor destroy
on all my holy mountain,
for the earth will be full of the knowledge of the Lord
as the waters cover the sea."[74]

To reconcile these passages 2 Peter 3 requires careful interpretation. The fiery imagery used by Peter is very powerful and evokes the Old Testament prophetic writings of judgement. These verses may well give us another dimension to the picture of a transformed earth – purified and cleansed by the fire of God's judgement[75] and holiness.

Further, the environmental disasters of Matthew 24 are described in a very interesting way, "All these are the beginning of birth-pains."[76] If the earth was truly on a downward path to destruction would Jesus not have described earthquakes and the like as "death-throes" rather than birth-pains?

Birth pains hurt, but there is new life at their end. The new life which Christ gave by his death has saved humanity from its sin and hopelessness. By the power of the Holy Spirit, he has restored the harmony of Creator and his image. In turn, this restored harmony enables the whole order of creation to be fulfilled. This brings us back to Romans 8 and creation waiting in eager expectation for "the sons of God to be revealed".[77] Again, we understand that these groanings represent "the pains of childbirth right up to the present time." Surely this reinforces the wonderful promise of transformation, but adds a measure of continuity. The link is once again made between humanity and the rest of creation, this time on two levels.

First, every Christian is aware that whilst it is wonderful to know God and have the "firstfruits of the Spirit", we long in frustration for that time when the completion of personal salvation will occur. Then there will be both physical transformation and spiritual fulfilment – the two are indivisible. Likewise, the whole creation experiences a similar frustration and a similar longing – its liberation is guaranteed but has not yet come.

The second and more direct link lies in the means of liberation. As humanity in Christ tastes "the glorious freedom of the children of God" - freedom *from* sickness, sin, decay; freedom *into* wholeness, eternal life and fulfilment – so the creation itself will be "brought into" this freedom. The Bible is rarely so interested in the "how" questions as in the "whys". We cannot say how this connection will be seen, but it is quite plain that as the *rebellion* of humanity in Adam and Eve caused the creation to be bound, so the *obedience* of humanity in Christ will cause its liberty.

But what about heaven? Heaven simply describes the place where God is. The classic Christian idea of life after death is that the deceased believer "goes to heaven", carrying with it the suggestion of leaving the earth behind. This belief is not so firmly secured in Scripture as might be thought. Not only do we have promises which apparently relate to *this* creation, but in the prophetic vision of Revelation 21 John,

"... saw the Holy City, the new Jerusalem, coming *down* out of heaven from God ..."[78] (my italics). John apparently saw that heaven was to be firmly located in the transformed physical universe which God had originally designed.

I was once in a consultation of evangelicals discussing the Bible and the environment. The subject of animals in the after-life came up and one speaker related how a preacher had told her that her cat was not going to heaven. A friend of mine piped up, "that's right, dear, he's coming back to earth to be with us!"

Betwixt and Between

With a joyful hope of fulfilment and "cosmic redemption" before us, what can we say about this present age? The coming of Jesus has brought great personal benefits for millions of believers down the centuries – fresh hope, forgiveness, healing and purpose. Through the work of Christian activists many social benefits have also been achieved: the Factory Acts, the abolition of slavery and prison reform.[79] But the past centuries have also seen an unparalleled level of human suffering, cruelty to animals and devastation of the environment.

The next chapter will examine why the gospel has made such little impact on our ecology to date. It will also look at the Kingdom of God, which means we live in the "already, but not yet", and how the Lord has given us eternal life – now.

Summary of Creation, Fall and Redemption

What we have firmly established so far is that the earth is the Lord's. That means all of it. Because God has made every living thing, whether animal, vegetable or mineral, it has its own intrinsic value. The myth that the worth of the creation can be measured on a sliding scale of its usefulness to humanity must be discarded. To speak of animal rights is misleading; these rights are God's as creator.

Humankind does have a leading role in the order of creation. This role is not one of a despotic dictator, lording it over the rest, but of a monarch, a first among equals. The original task assigned was to tend and to care for the rest of creation, shaping and developing its raw potential to reflect God's order. A heavy responsibility came with the post of monarch, and accountability was part of it.

Through their freewill, which was essential for people to have relationships, Adam and Eve chose the option of carving out their destiny apart from God. This led to spiritual death, fractured relationships and disorder in the creation. The presence of sin in humanity impacted the rest of creation to break its harmony.

God was not content with this sorry state of affairs. He sent his Son, Jesus, to become fully human but to remain fully God as well, and to live the model human life. More than this, he died as a substitute for every sinner who has lived and so enabled humanity's relations with God to be restored.

More that this yet, in breaking the power of sin and death Jesus not only redeemed people, but also the rest of creation. Only Satan and his angels, prejudged before time and space as we know it, are excluded from God's great work of salvation. So there is a great eschatological hope for the whole world – the whole order of created things. Heaven will come down to earth and the rule of God will be present in wholeness, peace and fulfilment. Heaven will not just be one long church meeting (phew!), but an adventure of creative exploration and fellowship with the living God.

In the last chapter of the Bible appears an image of the eternal life which Adam and Eve were offered in the first chapters: the tree of life. How fitting that this image should reflect and include the non-human creation which God so loves.

> "On each side of the river [of life] stood the tree of life, bearing twelve crops of fruit, yielding its fruit every month. And the leaves of the trees are for the healing of

the nations. No longer will there be any curse. The throne of God and of the Lamb will be in the city, and his servants will serve him.[80]

Notes

1 The parable can be found in Luke 15 and Matthew 18.
2 Genesis 6:6.
3 See Appendix 1.
4 See Genesis 9:1.
5 Genesis 9:3.
6 Genesis 9:5.
7 See Exodus 21:28.
8 Cf. Genesis 11:9 with 1:28 and 9:1.
9 Genesis 12:3b.
10 Eg Genesis 17:7; Exodus 6:7.
11 In fact, on account of Israel's unbelief and the consequent delay of the Jordan crossing, the Law was probably given some forty years before the conquest of Canaan began.
12 Galatians 3:24. Also see the incident from Jesus' life which so graphically demonstrates this truth in John 8:2–11.
13 These three paradigms are borrowed gratefully from Tim Cooper. See *Green Christianity*, *ibid.*, pp 57–61.
14 Eg see Joshua 7:14.
15 See 1 Kings 21:3.
16 See Leviticus 25 *passim*, especially vv 25–33. An example of this principle being exercised is given in Jeremiah 32:7,8, where the prophet is asked to redeem a field by his uncle.
17 Leviticus 25:21.
18 Vv 8–10.
19 Deuteronomy 22:10.
20 Deuteronomy 25:4.
21 Deuteronomy 22:4.
22 Exodus 20:10; 23:12.
23 Proverbs 12:10.
24 See *Atonement* in Appendix 1.
25 See Leviticus 17:11 and Hebrews 9:22
26 The passage from Ezekiel 36 quoted above is but one example.
27 Leviticus 20:22.
28 The evocative and emotional Psalm 137 is the best example.
29 The subject of dualism will be tackled in the next chapter.
30 Jeremiah 16:18.
31 Isaiah 2:4.

32 Isaiah 49:6.
33 Zechariah 9:9.
34 "Messiah" is the Hebrew word meaning "anointed one". "Christ" is the Greek form of the same word.
35 Matthew 10:29.
36 Matthew 6:26.
37 Matthew 6:28,29.
38 Mark 6:26–29.
39 "Kingdom of Heaven" (most frequently occurring in Matthew) and "Kingdom of God" are more or less synonymous phrases in the Gospels, denoting the rule and reign of God.
40 Matthew 13:31,32.
41 Matthew 13: 24–30.
42 Mark 13:28.
43 See Mark 6:38ff; Luke 24:43; John 21:1–14.
44 Eg Luke 22:7ff.
45 It is also told in Matthew 8:28ff and Luke 8:26ff.
46 CE Graham Swift *Mark* in *New Bible Commentary*, IVF, 1970, p 862.
47 Cf. Jesus' cleansing of the temple in John 2:13–17 and Matthew 21:12.
48 Another example which needs more than a first glance is Jesus' cursing of the fig-tree in Matthew 21:19.
49 2 Corinthians 5:19.
50 See Philippians 2:5–8 and 2 Corinthians 8:9.
51 Matthew 10:34.
52 John 4:1–26.
53 John 12:1–8.
54 Luke 8:1–3.
55 John 4:1–43, esp. v 43.
56 Luke 7:1–10.
57 Luke 11:52, 53.
58 Luke 16:19–31.
59 Matthew 19:16–24.
60 Eg those of Matthew 25: the ten virgins, the Talents, the sheep and the goats.
61 Luke 12:48.
62 Luke 4:18,19.
63 Matthew 5:17.
64 John 3:16.
65 Eg Vine, *ibid*. p 1256.
66 *Ibid*.
67 Galatians 6:28.
68 Galatians 3:13.
69 Hebrews 2:8.
70 Taken from the Greek, roughly translated eschatology means "a word about last things."
71 Revelation 21:1.

72 1 Corinthians 15:51,52.
73 John 19:30.
74 Isaiah 11:6–9.
75 The idea of a God of judgement is unfashionable in a sanitized age of comfort and compromise. The Bible tells us that God is slow to anger and quick to bless, but he hates sin, whilst loving every sinner. To make the principles of stewardship and responsibility meaningful, it is essential that there is justice in the end. The significance of Jesus' death in our place is that although actually guilty, those who have believed in him will be forgiven and will not face judgement for sin.
76 Verse 8.
77 Verse 19. The use of "sons" should not be considered exclusive gender language. Rather, the theme of the chapter is that those who are in Christ are adopted by the Father by the spirit of sonship. In a Roman household only the male children could be heirs (see verse 17).
78 Verse 2.
79 This is not to say that the record of Christianity in history has always been positive.
80 Revelation 22:2,3.

Chapter 6

WHERE ON EARTH IS THE CHURCH?

Recovering lost ground

The Missing Link

We have seen that the Bible is filled with positive images of the material environment of our world – quite literally from Genesis to Revelation. Creation is infinitely godly, marked everywhere with the Lord's fingerprints. The fall is complete in its terrible impact upon everything that has been made. Redemption is truly "cosmic", radically affecting *everything* in God's world: his beautiful arrangement of order.

Since all this is true, we must now ask why the Church has taken so long to develop an ecological conscience. I think that it is great to be alive and to know God today. I would not swap my place in time and history for anything. With the power of the Holy Spirit moving across every nation, and with high expectations of the Lord here in Britain, these are exciting days indeed. Many of the newer churches (and some older ones too!) have known the goodness of God pouring out freshness in worship, genuine supernatural signs and a high quality of church life. The gospel is being preached and many people with no church background are coming to experience the cleansing and healing of Jesus for the first time.

But there are some missing links. The lovely good news which God has given us is still rarely preached in a very green – that is, in a very whole – form. If the Bible is so clear on the goodness of the earth, why are its believers so reluctant to declare it? If this good news *is* good for everyone, why do we often make it difficult for those who care about the earth to receive it?

In Chapter 1, I outlined five roots of indifference to environmental awareness and action which apply to society in general. All of these will also apply to the Church, but there are others besides. Dave Tomlinson, has identified five key reasons for the Church's lack of response.[1]

1. Lack of balance between creation and fall

I have already suggested that liberal theologians have tended to over-emphasise Genesis 1 and 2 at the expense of Genesis 3: a denial of sin and its consequences distorts the goodness of God's creation, and its need of a saviour. Meanwhile, evangelicals have sometimes been guilty of the reverse: majoring on the fall and apparently forgetting the creation completely!

If we believe that the story really begins with a duff old sinful planet, it will seriously impact upon our motivation to care for the earth. The primary way in which we see the world – as something essentially good or as something ruined – radically affects our environmental interest. Of course, at present there is a paradox – the earth is both lovely and tainted with ugliness. However, through the lens of the Bible we are not left with such a tension forever. Even our hope-filled future looks back to the creation. Jesus described his future reign as the "*renewal*" - not the *replacement* – "of all things".[2]

2. Only visiting this planet

As we saw in the last chapter, some Christians are afflicted with a condition known as "eschatological gloom". They believe that in the end times the created world as we know it will be burned up in a final judgement while Christian believers depart for heaven. One particular version of this is known as "premillenial dispensationalism", and was first conceived in the last century by the Brethren leader, J N Darby. It has developed the idea of a "secret rapture" of believers, and an important role for national Israel. This view is widely held in some parts of the Church, especially among evangelicals in the USA. The end-product of dispensationalism is the belief that things are going to get steadily worse until Christ's return.

At least two major problems with this position are obvious. First, it encourages a kind of "departure lounge" mentality towards the earth. If we *are* only visiting this world, twiddling our proverbial thumbs and waiting for our Celestial Airways flight to wing us permanently to the next, we will hardly have much interest in renovating the airport! Second, if we expect things to get worse before this metaphorical 'plane departs for gloryland, we are in danger of wringing our hands gleefully when they do. The rain forest is smaller and the ozone hole is bigger, the end is a-coming!

This sort of eschatology flies in the face of biblical stewardship after the image of God. Again, it de-motivates the Church from positive inter-action with the creation. The scope of evangelism is restricted to rescuing people *out of* the world, rather than bringing wholeness *within* it. Saving souls is important, but it is only part of the full job.

3. Comfortable conservatism

This one could easily have come into Chapter 1 as it applies both within the Church and outside it. However, the Church in Britain is still largely middle-class, white and comfortable. If we were to look at our lifestyle and culture, there might be little to distinguish many Christians from our unbelieving neighbours. Tackling questions of world-view can have radical implications – it can seriously touch our structures and "invade our space"!

The status quo might be "the mess we're in", but many of us aren't doing too badly on a personal level. We might have more to lose if hard questions were to be asked about economic growth, home finances, science, technology and seeing green. In fact, some of us might actually be more inclined to see red! It has been suggested that perhaps this explains why prosperity teaching has been more popular over the past twenty years than environmental teaching.

However, the true follower of Christ has always been the one who truly follows Jesus' example; denying himself to take on "the very nature of a servant"[3] and living for God's agenda alone.

4. Suspected New Age infiltration of the green movement

The New Age movement is an important cultural trend which I want to look at more closely in Chapter 8. Over recent years it has gained a high level of notoriety – and caused quite a bit of hysteria – in the Church. This is largely because it is growing, is subtle and is a bit confusing!

Because many of its ideas are rooted in pantheism and Eastern religions, the New Age movement generally has a very high regard for the earth. The spirituality of the New Age movement has thus been very attractive to those who have got fed up with the materialism and the limitations of the technological age. Rejecting the "masculine", competitive and environmentally-nasty flavour of Western culture, Greens are naturally open to the more "feminine" and holistic worldview of the New Age.

From observation, and from common sense as well, it seems that what usually comes first is not New Age affiliation, but environmental awareness. This means that not all that is green is New Age. In fact, that assumption is a gross insult to the green Christian! Rather, the New Age movement seems to have filled a vacuum in our society from which the Church has largely retreated. This is part of the focus of a greener gospel.

5. Theological Dualism

There is a good sort and a bad sort of dualism.[4] It is helpful to rebuff monism – the theory that all reality is one. Monism is linked with pantheism and is thereby an essential part of the New Age package. We saw in Chapter 3 that at the heart of the Christian doctrine of creation is the separation between Creator and creatures. This dualism is fundamental to a biblical perspective. As well as standing against pantheism, it also denies that the moral battle between good and evil is a contest between equal and opposite forces.[5] God is eternal and exists by his own power: Satan and his demons are all fallen creatures whose destiny has been sealed.[6]

However, the idea that there are also dualisms *within* the creation is one of the most dangerous concepts to have hit the Church. Many people are convinced that this is the greatest flaw in Western Christianity today. Dualism is certainly an active ingredient in each of the other factors outlined above. Two Canadian thinkers, Brian Walsh and Richard Middleton, put the problem down to our worldview.[7] They claim that a variety of dualisms are central to the Western worldview.

How green is your worldview?

A worldview is the map and compass which helps us to interpret reality. It enables us to steer through the often murky and complex waters of life, relationships and the Bible itself.

As far as dualistic worldviews are concerned, they are based on the Greek philosophies of neo-Platonism. These ideas were picked up and re-interpreted during the Age of Reason by Rene Descartes and other deists. In Chapter 3, I noted that it was this period of "Enlightenment" which so radically affected the formation of the industrial and technological society as we know it. A dualistic separation of matter/spirit and public/private has profoundly affected our whole way of thinking and working out values.

Take, for example, the political world. In a democracy, men and women are placed in power because enough people believe that they will keep the promises which they have made in public. If they do not keep election promises they will usually be kicked out by the voters. However, if they commit adultery and are unfaithful to the more private promises they have made to their partner, this is less of a problem. They might have to lie low for a while but it is unlikely to ruin them.[8] The public and the private are treated as two totally separate realms.

Unfortunately, a Christian *worldview* may be different from a truly *biblical worldview* – indeed it could lie closer to a *dualistic worldview.* We are all deeply influenced by our surroundings and unless we are truly open to the power of the Holy Spirit, and to the challenge of God's word, we will interpret Scripture through the lens of our worldview. This is why the Bible commands,

> "Do not conform any longer to the pattern of this world, but be transformed by the renewing of your mind."[9]

The tense used in the second phrase is the present continuous, so literally becomes, "by the *continual* renewing of your mind". We should constantly be allowing the Lord to re-shape our worldview. I think of the way I saw the world ten years ago – through prejudice, through hypocrisy, through limited vision – and I was *already* a Christian then. If the Lord has changed my mind and changed my whole outlook once, he has done it a hundred times. What is more, I hope I will be able to say the same thing in another ten years! To rephrase the Heineken advert, "only God can do this".

Upstairs, Downstairs

When we come to look at the church, dualism is certainly a potent force. Put simply, the world is often viewed in a kind of "upstairs, downstairs" way. For example, many separations have been read into Christianity over the centuries: Soul and body; flesh and spirit; sacred and secular; holy and worldly; heaven and earth. To make a distinction is one thing, to push it to extremes is quite another.

One of the best examples of this is presented in a profound sociological study of the subject by Adrian Plass. In his diary, he describes a visit to his house by two characters, known as Mr and Mrs Flushpool,

"Mrs Flushpool described at great length how she had been converted from fleshly works and appetites since being washed in the blood, and how, in consequence, she was now able to turn her back on those things that she used to do in what she called "the natural". Everything she said seemed to have a kind of dampness about it. She and her husband refused wine, saying that Christians should be ashamed to have it in the house, as it led to carnal excess. At this point, Mr Flushpool let out another sonorous, "Amen to that!" Coffee was also frowned on as something that was wont to stimulate inappropriately in the natural.

"Gerald, with a perfectly straight face, asked Mrs Flushpool if she used to go swimming in the natural. She replied fervently that her bodily flesh would never again rouse any man to a fever of sensual lust.

"Mr Flushpool opened his mouth very wide to say, "Amen to that!" but thought twice and shut it".[10]

When I was a new Christian, I was also confused about some of these contrasts. Some were obvious and not a problem – I knew that my old body was going to die, and that my soul would live on in a new one. The difference between soul and body is real enough (although not quite as extreme as we sometimes think!). What really puzzled me was the language of getting "out of the natural" and "into the spiritual". When enthusiastically praising God in church meetings, I was told I must make sure I was dancing "in the Spirit", and not "in the flesh". What was this mysterious contrast? From careful observation, I could not be sure whether I was supposed to feel something different inside, or just hop about gracelessly with glazed eyes fixed on the middle distance.

Then there was spirit and emotions. Highly influenced as I was by the writings of the Chinese mystic, Watchman Nee, I realised that I was supposed to analyse my feelings. Was my love for Charlotte "soulish" or "soulical" - ie, was it just natural or inspired by the Holy Spirit? What was all this about? I was beginning to feel that there was a kind of spiritual schizophrenia abroad in the Church. I could not live my life in such black and white terms, and put myself under great pressure trying to do so.

True, in Paul's letters we do read of the flesh (or "sinful nature" in the NIV) and the spirit. The Greek word translated "flesh" and "sinful nature" is *sarx*, another of those with many different meanings.[11] When used negatively, as for example in Galatians 6:8, *sarx* speaks of the weaker element of human nature or the seat of sin in man.[12] It should not be read as a wholly self-contained part of the human make up, and it certainly should not be confused with the body. We have already seen that humanity, along with all creation, stands in the paradox of being wonderfully made and yet tragically fallen. It is neither right nor helpful (although it does satisfy the rational mind!) to push these two elements to separate extremes of black and white. The Bible does not deny the shades of grey which we see in the present reality.

Instead, the concepts of body, soul, spirit and so on should be seen positively as all being part of the wholeness of a person. We might recognise that, for example, our body is conscious of the world, our emotions are conscious of our self and our spirits are conscious of God, but how can we separate these experiences completely? Developing wholeness in every area of life – work, hobbies, relationships, worships, etcetera – are essential to being fully rounded people, and involve equally our minds, spirits and bodies.

Dualism at large

Avoiding dualism in our personal walk with God can help our sanity, but there is more to it than this. If Christians are taught to separate the realms of "the spiritual" and "the natural", it is a short step to separating the public from the private and the church from the home, the college, the business, the sports club and so on. In this day and age you would hardly find an evangelical who would admit to being a "Sunday Christian", one who goes to church but does not live a Christian life. However, because our worldview is so heavily affected by dualism in reality, we find that our words and our actions often fail to add up.

This is why dualism is dangerous: it not only discourages a positive view of the earth, but it can discredit the entire Christian message. While there is a gulf between what we *say we believe*, and what we *actually believe* there is unlikely to be much dynamic Acts 2 discipleship around. Just as it was in Jerusalem after Pentecost, so the world is now looking for a message that is credible.

On top of this, dualism will rob us of a right theological outlook in many areas. For example, in the last chapter I looked at the link between God's people and the land. A denial of the spiritual value of matter means that we may fail to see the significance of "the land" of Palestine as a physical territory ("spiritualising" it instead); the inheritance of the earth by the meek and Abraham claiming the same hill of Moriah in Genesis 22 that Jesus died upon. It will also lead us to deny that God wants bodies, not just spirits, and that Jesus walked in harmony with the earth, recognising its goodness (for example, by eating wheat) as well as its manifestations of sin.

At the thinner end of the dualism wedge lies a tendency to bring a vertical hierarchy into the church. In the new humanity of Galatians 3 and Ephesians 2, the priesthood of all believers[13] serve the Lord together. We must beware of dualistic ideas of clergy and laity, full-timers and the congregation, creeping into the hearts of our churches.

Two realms or two regimes?

One of the clearest ways of sorting out the false separations which humans have invented, from the created distinctions as God made different each thing "after its kind"[14] has been produced by Albert Wolters.[15] He draws a box to show some of creation's major areas, pointing out that church life is different from family life and so on. The lines between each of the areas are God-ordained and they do not divide the creation. Figure A shows this model.

Figure A: CREATION

church

family

politics

business

art

education

journalism

thought

emotion

plants and animals

inanimate matter

What we are observing, however, often follows something like the pattern of Figure B. When we see the world as divided into two realms horizontally, the danger is that we identify a "first class bit" of creation, of humanity or so on, and a "second class bit".

Figure B: TWO REALMS

The kingdom of God (sacred)	church
	family
	politics
	business
"the world"	art
(secular)	education
	journalism
	thought
	emotion
	plants and animals
	inanimate matter

Rather than two *realms*, a sort of Happy Valley on the one hand and a Grumpyville on the other, the Bible identifies two *regimes* – both battling for the same territory, leaving nothing neutral. This brings us back to the first paragraph of the chapter, seeing that God has made everything, sin has touched everything and Christ has redeemed everything. The picture will look very different.

Figure C: TWO REGIMES

chu rch

fami ly

politi cs

busin ess

the kingdom of God ar t *"the world"*

edu cation

tho ught

emot ion

plants an d animals

inanima te matter

Figure C shows that the battle lines are jagged, not straight: Different areas experience differing degrees of liberation or bondage (to use Romans 8 language). In contrast to a *dualistic worldview*, this model offers an integral or *wholistic worldview*. Nothing is hived off – salvation will touch everything apart from Satan and God himself.

Summary

Given all this, the Christian should not be seeking to "get upstairs" - to deny the natural in favour of the spiritual or to emphasise the church as against the world. To value wrestling in prayer more highly than battling against pollution, or preaching more than politics, will clearly affect our environmental response. More than this, it will also say a lot about how limited or broad is our view of what Jesus has done on the Cross.

There is only one true antidote to the dualism which grips our culture and too often grips the Church. The one way to secure a properly wholistic worldview is, not surprisingly, there in the Bible itself. It is the concept of the Kingdom of God. Far more than the Church, only an understanding of God's reign and rule can truly equip us to live out an wholistic life, and fulfil the great commission to . . .

> ". . . go into all the world and preach the good news to all creation".[16]

This Kingdom is the focus of the next Chapter.

Notes

1 These were set out as part of a lecture to the Christian Ecology Link conference, Cliff College, 6 July 1991.
2 Matthew 19:28.
3 Philippians 2:7.
4 A dualism exists when there are two powers or elements which are totally separate and independent.
5 For example, this would describe the Zoroastrian belief.
6 See Revelation 20 and cf. Luke 10:18.
7 See Walsh and Middleton *The Transforming Vision* IVP, 1984.
8 This scenario was adequately illustrated by events surrounding the leader of a British political party in February, 1992.
9 Romans 12:2.
10 *The Sacred Diary of Adrian Plass* Marshall Pickering 1987, p 81.
11 Vine has identified at least thirteen. See WE Vine, *ibid.*, pp 447,448.
12 *Ibid.*
13 See 1 Peter 2:5,9.
14 Genesis 1:11ff.
15 The following tables are all gratefully borrowed from Albert M Wolters *Creation Regained* IVP, 1985, pp 63-66.
16 Mark 16:15.

PART THREE

WHAT CAN WE DO?

Chapter 7

THE PEACE OF THE LORD

The Kingdom and *Shalom*

Reaching for the Kingdom

It is quite impossible to understand the Church, or any part of its role in the earth, unless we first understand the Kingdom. The Kingdom of God is the rule and reign of King Jesus on the earth in this age, as a foretaste of what it will be like in the age to come.[1] Jesus was certainly preoccupied with the subject of the Kingdom while he walked the earth, but offered no simple definition of it. His phrase, "what shall I say the Kingdom of God is like?"[2] suggests that the Kingdom will always be greater and more wonderful than we can ever grasp.

However, certain characteristics are quite clear. For all I have said about geography, the biblical idea of the Kingdom is not of a realm. Instead, the Greek word *basileia* suggests more of the activity of ruling. This interpretation reinforces the worldview presented in the last chapter. If the Kingdom is wholistic we must not merely seek a cocoon-like *realm* of God's reign, but rather the *regime* of God's rule in the *totality* of his creation. Naturally, this regime will affect territory: whether a literal location, like the county of Devon, or another category like architecture or farming. That is why the third diagram in the last chapter showed a jagged line – some parts of creation show more of God's Kingdom than others.

A New Testament concept which runs parallel to that of the Kingdom is *zoe* – the Greek word translated, "eternal life". This is the preferred phrase of the gospel-writer John, and picks up the thought of the Kingdom and God's life bridging this age and the age to come. Resurrection life is not something for which Christians need to wait. It does not arrive after death, but we will rise from death because God gave us his *zoe* when we first repented and believed in Christ. This explains why Jesus pointed Martha away from the distant future and towards his presence as they approached the tomb of Lazarus. "I *am* the resurrection and the life. He who believes in me will live . . ."[3]

Far more than just a future reality then, Jesus constantly reminded his listeners that the Kingdom was "at hand"[4] (or "within reach"[5]). This exquisite phrase conjures up the dual ideas of the immediacy of God's Kingdom on the one hand, and the need for it to be received on the other. In an attempt to unlock these truths, writers have come up with a number of ways to describe it. Some bright spark once coined the phrase that the Kingdom is "already, but not yet". It is upon us, but not at this time in its full and final expression. George Eldon Ladd said that we live in "the presence of the future". These notions translate the prayer ". . . your Kingdom come . . ."[6] from passive contemplation to "standing on the tiptoes of faith"[7] to preach the good news and live the good news, that the Kingdom might somehow come through us.

Such a healthy view of the Kingdom keeps our churches on track. We are not so absorbed with the present that we have no hope of the wonderful promised inheritance – our future rule and reign with Christ. Yet neither are we so consumed with the future that we lose motivation to get involved with the world and become embroiled in what Roger Ellis calls "sci-fi eschatology". Ladd said that the basic demand of the Kingdom is a response of man's will. This choice will lead us to a commitment to co-operate with the Holy Spirit in sharing the good news of the Kingdom, living ethically according to the values of the Kingdom, and of course praying for the final coming of the Kingdom.

The Kingdom and the Earth[8]

I believe that the Kingdom of God should require a

thoroughly wholistic and green way of life. If living in the Kingdom is about submitting to King Jesus and becoming a partner of the Holy Spirit in getting God's will done, we will want to ask how this affects our relationship with the whole earth. To help us, let's now consider some other characteristics of the Kingdom.

1. A Kingdom of Power

Power was the promise of Jesus to his disciples whilst they awaited the Holy Spirit[9] which brought the "down-payment" of their eternal inheritance.[10] The work of Jesus during his earthly ministry was filled with dynamic demonstrations of God's power breaking into situations. Healings and deliverance were commonplace and even his teaching was filled with such authority that his listeners were amazed.[11] We rejoice that God is restoring to us these signs of the power of his Kingdom in the Church today.

But what could this mean for a Church seeking to recover a wider role as the agent of God's Kingdom? If the Kingdom is truly about ushering in the age to come, which will bring the restoration of all things, then surely there has to be some good news in this for the earth.

The main message of this book is hopefully becoming clearer: as Christians we have a duty as God's people to care about what God cares about, and that includes the earth itself. As the Kingdom is at hand, we seek to grab handfuls of heaven to share Jesus with our friends and our towns, to live a more whole and clean life by the power of the Spirit and to heal the sick as Jesus did.

Surely we need to be grabbing handfuls of the age to come for the rest of creation as well. In the first chapter I mentioned that one of the main "turn-offs" which affect the green movement is a feeling of powerlessness in the face of massive ecological problems. Knowing that we are working towards the Kingdom, Christians should reach out for God's power to strengthen their resolve to add to the solutions, rather than to the problems.

More than this, are we open to the power of the Kingdom

breaking through in a truly supernatural way? God might well want to show his power by doing something spectacular with the ozone hole, the atmospheric temperature or the spread of deserts. If only we are willing to pray, "your Kingdom come". Maybe this seems too far off the wall, but let's remember the magnificent words that Jesus left us,

> I tell you the truth, anyone who has faith in me will do what I have been doing. He will do even greater things than these, because I am going to the Father.[12]

2. A Kingdom of Righteousness

As far as God is concerned the wholism of the Kingdom will cut both ways. If you are interested in the environment as a Christian, you may well have been told by someone that the Lord cares more about what is going on inside of you, than what is happening outside. In other words, don't waste time worrying about the earth, just make sure you are living a righteous life.

Meanwhile, I frequently hear green Christians berating those brothers and sisters who do not have their energy or belief in the environmental cause. One could be forgiven for thinking that in their motivation to care for the earth they had actually found an alternative righteousness. At worst this can produce a green pharisaism, or a "greener than thou" attitude, imposing guilt rather than spreading good news.

A "Kingdom Green" will reject both these expressions of dualism. Righteousness is a fundamental demand of the Kingdom: "seek first the Kingdom *and its righteousness*"[13] was Jesus' exhortation. Whilst we have been made righteous by the forgiveness and cleansing of Christ's blood, there is still a righteousness we must seek and for which we must "hunger and thirst."[14] Reading through Jesus' teaching of the so-called Sermon on the Mount in Matthew's gospel,[15] it becomes plain that this righteousness is a reflection of the morality and integrity of the King whom we follow.

Of course, personal morality is more than a complete end

in itself. I believe that there is so much to do in the Kingdom that monastic isolation from the real world has little to commend it in the long term. However, Christianity is an "inside-out" faith: it's what God works into us that we must work out in our lives.[16] If I run away from my past, my weaknesses and the choking habitual sins which trip me up when I want to do good, I will hardly be able to bring true wholeness to the earth!

This is where the Church comes into its own. Amongst a body of people who are seeking the Kingdom together, we can share our secrets, however negative, and pray and support one another as we all ask the Holy Spirit to make us more like Jesus. Again, this will do more than just make us feel happier with life, it will add to our credibility. If we are to finally reject the dualism of saying that we believe in one thing, but actually living out another, something must happen on the inside and be worked out in the world. Private morality and social justice will be seen as equal priorities.

3. A Kingdom of Justice

The cry for justice rose to God from the earliest days of post-fall history. Enshrined in the Law of Moses and repeated tirelessly by the prophets, Jesus demonstrated that justice was to be a key ingredient in the coming Kingdom of God. In what has been described as the manifesto of his Messianic ministry, he took up the words of the prophet Isaiah in proclaiming his mission in the synagogue at Nazareth.[17] In the midst of his proclamation of the ". . . year of the Lord's favour . . .",[18] the words "freedom", "liberty" and "release" stand out boldly in his message.

Once again this evokes the words of Romans 8 and the longed-for liberation of creation from its bondage. To live as Kingdom people we must face the challenge of being those who participate in this liberation of creation, rather than in its bondage. What a firm foundation stone on which to build a Christian environmental ethic! Seeking justice should affect our treatment of animals, our attitude towards pollution, and the thoughtless plundering of nature's wealth.

However, I have already stated my belief that to be green affects far more than just the way we interact with the non-human creation. Whilst striving for ecological justice on the one hand, green Christians should also be in the forefront of social action, evangelism, prayer and human rights on the other. Within a wholistic worldview, all these dimensions promote Kingdom justice.

4. A Kingdom of Reconciliation

Jesus' parable of the lost son opens up what is surely one of the most powerful and inspiring elements of the good news of the Kingdom.[19] How many of us can relate to the young prodigal who wants to blow his inheritance on the glittering offers of the world system? Many more of us will also have painful memories of the pig's-ear mess we had made of lives, and the proverbial pig's-sty in which we lived when Father God found us. Yet the unconditional forgiveness of the Father to his profligate child, reconciling that lost individual by his loving grace, is where all Christians begin to construct a new life.

Wonderfully, God does not leave it there. He wants us to be involved in his wider purpose of "reconciling the world to himself in Christ"[20] by giving us "the ministry of reconciliation".[21] As we saw from the fall, the primary work of sin and Satan has been to fracture the harmony of God's world and particularly of God's image, humanity. This disharmony soon brought outright division: man against woman, man against man, man against God, man against nature and so on. As sin and division entered the world through humanity, so did its antidote: reconciliation.

Because the gospel of the Kingdom is good news, wherever Jesus is received reconciliation will be present. Restored relationships, mended marriages and healed family feuds will all be associated with entering into God's Kingdom. When people find that they have been cleaned up and restored to God it's hardly surprising that this reconciliation becomes infectious. The Kingdom must see all the barriers that separate race, colour, gender, and all minority groups dissolved in healing, forgiveness and repentance. Jesus has become the last word on dealing with every such bar,

> "For he himself is our peace, who has made the two one and has destroyed the barrier, the dividing wall of hostility . . ."[22]

In Luke's account of Jesus' words of commission to his disciples in Acts 1:8, he tells them that they will be his "witnesses in Jerusalem, and in all Judea and Samaria, and to the ends of the earth". The Church has historically put a priority on sending out the zealous to the ends of the earth.[23] Local churches that are growing will be working on their immediate vicinity – their Jerusalem. Increasingly, God is speaking about church-planting: reaching the Judea that each of us have on our doorsteps. But where is our Samaria? Could this mean going to our traditional enemies, to seek them out with the reconciling message of the Kingdom? Whether that enemy be a personal rival or a national group, the Christian and the Church is mandated to "go and make disciples . . ."[24] and to be agents of reconciliation.

Meanwhile, the Kingdom is not being expressed whilst there is a lack of true relational unity in the body of Christ, whether between Catholic and Protestant, English and Scot, black and white, North and South or whatever other labels may exist. It's time for the Church to demonstrate something far more radical of the Kingdom of reconciliation.

In Chapter 3, we saw that there are two distinct categories within reality: God himself and the rest of creation. As the Kingdom touches humanity, so reconciliation must extend to all creation. Jesus' vision was of the "renewal of all things"[25] – he clearly intended that believers' new found restoration and reconciliation to God would touch their dealings with the whole of the earth. Far more than a token idea of "being nice to nature", this attitude must have the vigour and dynamism of every other aspect of Kingdom life. It is close to the biblical idea of *shalom*, a Hebrew word inadequately translated in English as "peace".

The Fruit of the Kingdom

In terms of humanity's response to the rest of creation, I want to add *shalom* to the two paradigms, or models, of dominion and stewardship which were discussed earlier. The link with the Kingdom is plain: *shalom* must be a fruit of the Kingdom.

> For the Kingdom of God is . . . righteousness, peace and joy in the Holy Spirit, because anyone who serves Christ in this way is pleasing to God and approved by men.[26]

When we think of peace, it usually brings to mind a negative idea. It is generally thought of as the *absence* of something – conflict, turmoil, fear or war. Peace is generally considered as fragile and temporary, typified by Neville Chamberlain's ironic 1938 declaration of "peace in our time". Alternatively, peace might conjure up some hippy concept of passive inactivity. On the cult children's television programme of the 1970s, The Magic Roundabout, life happens at high speed around Dylan the hippy rabbit whilst he is simply slumped against a tree uttering, "peace, man"!

In contrast, both *shalom* and its Greek counterpart, *eirene* are quite the opposite – positive, firm, permanent and full of life. *Shalom* does, of course, involve a rejection of violence, and adopting an opposite spirit to that of the world, but the primary meaning of the word implies wholeness, health, prosperity and completeness. In Joshua 8:31 it is used of an uncut stone, in Nehemiah 6:15 of the completed Jerusalem wall and in Isaiah 42:19 (AV) of a servant who has been "made perfect".[27] In this context, the notion that peace is a central fruit of the Kingdom offers us another angle on the wholistic nature of the gospel.

Further, *shalom* will turn an wholistic worldview into

action. We have seen that the Genesis 1:28 idea of dominion explains humanity's role in harnessing nature and bringing it to fulfilment, whilst Genesis 2:15 introduces the more caring dimension of stewardship, based on accountability to God. *Shalom*, however, must overarch both of these paradigms. Only if we understand the fact that creation is a whole, and that the Kingdom restores that healthy completeness, will we be in the right place to take positive steps forward.

Living for the Kingdom

I began this chapter by saying that only an understanding of the Kingdom could explain the Church. The contrasting truth is that there would be little evidence of the Kingdom if not for the Church. It is the Church whose calling is to proclaim the good news of the Kingdom in words, works and wonders. It holds the keys of the Kingdom[28] and therefore is able to unlock it to others – or keep it locked up![29] Only a healthy emphasis on the broad scope of the Kingdom of God will enable the Church to maintain a proper focus on the world in which it is located. No one has expressed this more articulately than Howard Snyder,

> "The Church gets into trouble whenever it thinks it is in the church-business rather than the Kingdom-business. In the church-business people are concerned with church activities, religious behaviour and spiritual things. In the Kingdom-business, people are concerned with Kingdom activities, all human behaviour and everything that God has made, visible and invisible. Church-people think about how to get people into the Church, Kingdom-people think about how to get the Church into the world. Church-people worry that the world might change the Church, Kingdom-people work to see the Church change the world!"[30]

Once again, the whole green agenda is not something that can be merely tacked onto the end of our Christian beliefs, activities and conferences. Part of the armour of God is the "readiness that comes with the gospel of peace."[31] To live out *shalom* involves a commitment to a complete and radical life. It requires a readiness to bring to bear that opposite spirit whenever we see an opportunity to resist the kingdom of darkness and introduce God's health. This readiness also carries with it an obligation to act. Of all people, Christians should be those who are able to think globally and act locally. All local churches should be seeking to work this out.

Finally, to be armed with the gospel of *shalom* will also require a willingness to be self-sacrificial, to evaluate and challenge the ways in which we use resources and spend our money. In the final chapter I want to consider how the individual can respond to the challenge of *shalom* – living with particular reference to the environment. I have also prepared some worksheets to enable groups to get started with action on the ground.[32] However, as this chapter has focussed on the Church and the Kingdom, I want to close with a look at the corporate responses churches can make.

Educate

The importance of doctrine is that what we believe influences what we do. Our examination of dualism showed that how we live will be the true acid test to sort out what we believe from what we say we believe. Therefore the role of teaching in the church is primary. Hopefully this book, along with others like it, will make a small contribution to the resourcing of church leaders in tying a clear green perspective into a robust Jesus-based and Kingdom-based theology.

However, the biblical material does need to be taught thoroughly in the local church context. Only then can materialism and dualism be exposed; creation, fall and redemption understood, and the Christian hope fully grasped. Of all these aspects, perhaps the doctrine of creation is most needy of profile in our churches. A clear knowledge of this subject is essential as a foundation to an environmental perspective and as a basis to refute the monistic myths of the New Age worldview.

With the subjects of both creation and heaven, recent teaching has sadly revolved more around controversies than around positive revelation. Let's recapture the minds of this generation by declaring boldly the two fixed points of the Christian worldview: where we came from and where we are going.

Evaluate[33]

If we are to take seriously the implications of a more wholistic approach to our faith, we will need to evaluate, and re-evaluate some of our present language, methods and values.

1) Language

In terms of our vocabulary, some of our best-loved words and phrases are given far too narrow a meaning. The most obvious example is "gospel". As we have seen in this chapter, the good news of the Kingdom is so much more than just words; it should contain all the qualities of the Kingdom of God itself. If a gospel is preached which does not demand social justice (eg restitution of financial wrongs), personal righteousness (eg a more Christ-like morality) and *shalom* with the earth (eg a review of our leisure, transport and spending habits), it is surely deficient. Likewise, the power of the Holy Spirit must be in the midst of our proclamation of the gospel.

Closely related to the gospel is the word "evangelism". The idea of "getting people saved" is not one of which we should be ashamed, because people need salvation. But if evangelism is a proclamation of the good news of the Kingdom, how are we communicating this good news? We live in a visual age and we need to communicate visually. As Mike Morris says, this involves more than using an overhead projector to illustrate a sermon! We desperately need to evaluate what we are modelling to our communities through our corporate witness. Happily, many churches are currently drawing together the concepts of social involvement and evangelism in a more wholistic way. Instead of seeing the two separately we recognise that both are integral to being salt and light in the earth. The next question is whether there is any good news for the earth in our evangelism!

There are many other ways in which we need to evaluate our language. "Going to heaven" is hardly a helpful phrase if you agree with the redemption of this earth. The Church is notorious for its jargon and clichés; the way to reduce this is to ensure that believers are aware of what is meant by such phrases as "the Kingdom", "wholistic" and "eschatology". The link between the process of evaluation and education is thus key.

2) Buildings

Owned premises are often a mixed blessing as far as local churches are concerned. They provide a focal point in the community and guarantee a meeting place, but can be restrictive in size and prohibitive in maintenance costs. When an environmental dimension is introduced, those churches which do own buildings have an opportunity and a responsibility to lead their communities by example. Energy conservation, cleaning products used, recycling facilities on the premises, care for the churchyard – all these questions have a very practical impact in fleshing out the message of a greener gospel.

Further, are the premises being used as a resource to the wider community? The idea of a religious building where God lives and in which you would only show your face if you fancied a bit of religion is anathema to the Kingdom of God. In a culture of isolation and loneliness barriers within the community could be brought down by the effective shared use of this resource.

3) Other Resources

Even churches which do not have their own premises are likely to use some resources. Letters, newsheets, etcetera could be printed on recycled paper and all used paper should be recycled. The needs of vegetarians and non-caffeine drinkers should be catered for, and non-disposable crockery used at events wherever possible. Where a church lets office space, the policies described above could be put into effect with those facilities.

4) Investments

I have left a whole chapter to consider the question of money, but in this context the question of invested finance cannot be ignored. Church funds could be invested in "ethically sound" trusts which may not guarantee the highest return, but give value to more important issues. Further, churches could give some of their finances to aid and justice agencies, thus expressing a desire to see the global North/South inequalities redressed.

For example, in Revelation, we are seeking to pursue a different model of transferring resources to poorer parts of the world. Relationships have been developed with two church leaders in struggling situations: one in Romania and another in Zaire. Through these men, whom we have visited and now know and trust, we have been able to send considerable aid of various sorts to support their own development projects. Naturally, many other churches are developing similar opportunities.

5) Transport

As the motor car is one of the single-most important contributors to pollution in our society we have got to do some hard thinking about this question. Where public transport is conveniently available, let's publicise it and encourage its use. We must stop to think about making journeys with only one or two people in the car. Can we share a car, or a journey regularly?

Certainly, churches do need to consider their locations carefully. Are they meeting in a place which is geographically accessible to the community? Are the leaders walking or cycling to the meetings?!

6) The Social Ecology

Evaluate the social ecology of your church, in other words the way in which the individuals relate together and welcome others. Our local churches must manifest the health and wholeness of the Kingdom if we are to reach our communities with the good news of the Kingdom. Questions such as the role and leadership of women, whether leadership adequately reflects the ethnic and social mix of the congregation, catering for special needs (those with hearing, visual and other disabilities) can have far-reaching significance.

Exercise

The process of evaluating our present situation should clearly lead us to action in our local churches. As with all new emphases that God brings to us, it is important to ask the questions with an openness to the Lord, being aware that all resources – time, finance, people – need to be prioritised. Once we have made a commitment to live out *shalom* we will then be ready to work out precisely what that means for us.

However, an internal response is only part of our ability to take corporate action. If the Kingdom means getting the Church into the world, we will want to consider how we *exercise* this principle with reference to the environment.

1) Political channels

During the 1980s, the question of the political neutrality of the Church frequently spilled over into controversy. The classic dualism of one brand of politics was expressed most clearly in 1984 when junior Government minister John Butcher called on the clergy to give up politics for Lent and "concentrate on their major tasks of saving souls and filling churches".[35] Whilst some churches do need more than a gentle reminder about the priority of evangelism, I have sympathy with the Bishop of Coventry's reply that, "politics is too important to be left to politicians"![36]

It is critically important that churches are in touch with

their local MPs, MEPs and Councils about environmental issues. From my experience, many politicians are pleasantly surprised that churches want to play their part. In fact, when I wrote to our local MP on behalf of Revelation recently to urge a more ecologically-sound disposal of sewage waste, he thanked me profusely saying it was "helpful ammunition" to take to the local water authority! By the way, I always remind him that as a church we pray for him as he seeks to govern diligently on our behalf.

Writing to the local authorities representing the views of 50 or 500 residents can have a mighty impact, as can writing letters to the local newspaper. These are all forms of political action which do not involve you marching in protest or chaining yourselves to the railings, although who knows . . .

2) Protest and Pressure

Some people will want to get more heavily dedicated to environmental action and we are familiar with the other pressure groups in this sphere. Certainly, to show some interest as a church in say, the local Friends of the Earth group would provide a valuable window into the community for the church, and would hopefully positively affect the group.

It has been said that as Christians our ethics will be based on doing what is right not for what can be achieved but because we live our lives before God. Whilst this is true, our ethics will make a difference. For example, protest does actually work. A geomorphologist known to me was talking to the senior exploration geologist in one of the top ten global oil companies last year. "We don't drill in jungles any more," he moaned. Instead of complaining about costs and overheads he continued, "It's environmental pressure. D**n Sierra Club freaks"![37]

3) Consumer power

All church-goers are also consumers, as is the church itself. Making contact with the local retailers to find out which shops stock the most ecologically-sound products and then using these will be a very practical part of our witness. I have nagged our local freezer shop to stock free-range and organic produce; complained to supermarket managers about wasted packaging and congratulated a local electrical shop for selling low-watt light bulbs. Why should shopping be impersonal and soul-less? We must make the connection between our own choices and the health of the global environment.

If this inter-action with shop-keepers was put onto a church level, I am sure that results would soon follow.

4) Spiritual Warfare

Recognising the reality of the angelic realm and its inter-relatedness to life on earth is part of a yet broader ecological theology. Within evangelical churches in Britain and the US, spiritual warfare has become one of the buzz issues of the 1990s. Whilst there is no space here to develop this subject properly, the Church has clearly been given authority over the works of darkness.[38] With the insight and discernment that comes from the Holy Spirit, we must engage in the kind of spiritual warfare envisaged in Ephesians 6:10–20.

If the Kingdom is about proclaiming and bringing in the rule of Christ, it must also involve displacing the present usurper, Satan and his powers. Bishop and Droop[39] argue that the way in which we engage in this warfare is to declare "the manifold wisdom of God" to "the rulers and authorities in the heavenly realms."[40] They say that as Satan has somehow "energised" the disobedient (Ephesians 2:2) so his powers have energised the structures and social orders of society. As we pray and proclaim the fact of their defeat at Calvary, the powers must give ground.

This is one model of many to help us understand how we can "wrestle . . . against spiritual wickedness in high places."[41] Few would argue that there is not something demonic in the grip of multinationals upon Third World economies and the arms industry, let alone the pornography and gambling industries. We have been given the Holy Spirit and the armour of God to pull down Satan's strongholds in the earth and we must exercise our spiritual authority.

Summary

In the second part of this chapter, I have thrown out a number of questions which churches must face. Few church leaders will feel they have no room for improvement (author definitely included!) but asking the right questions is as important as having the right answers.

We are privileged as God's Church to be the custodians of his wonderful Kingdom. This Kingdom will bring the most radical transformation the earth has ever seen. Let's see that we live out all its qualities and make Jesus very happy.

Practical Steps

- Write down your own statement of the good news of the Kingdom in one sentence. Is it wholistic and does it have the Ephesians 6:15 quality of peace? Is this gospel in any way different to what you have proclaimed to your friends?
- Organise a "Creation Day" in your community. We need to be imaginative in our evangelism, and express the fact that we have a greener gospel. By holding an outdoor event with music, drama and short preached messages all based around the theme of creation, you may be surprised at the interest you arouse. Plan it well, advertise it and let me know how it goes!
- If your church owns a building or has its own office, ask your leaders, minister or priest if you can undertake a "green audit" of the premises. Consider the following issues:

- is the churchyard managed properly; could it be used more effectively as a "green lung" in your town (see address for information in Appendix 2); could part of it be set aside as a haven for wildlife;[42] if the ground is covered in asphalt, could this be restored to vegetation; are there other areas where trees could be planted?

– does your church have a good energy conservation policy? Low-energy lightbulbs, proper insulation and time-switches will save money and reduce greenhouse emissions. Re-use cardboard boxes and packages, avoid all aerosols (the non-CFC ones still release greenhouse gases) and use pottery and glass cups instead of disposable (and non-biodegradable!) plastic ones. We need to break the habits of our disposable culture.

– are the cleaning products and other "household goods" used environment-friendlier and recycled?

– is the waste paper, glass, postage stamps, silver foil and aluminium, etc. recycled? If there are no recycling schemes in the area, could the church start one?

– is the paper used in the office recycled?

– can you spot other ways of greening the premises?

• Do an environmental-awareness survey of your congregation. Ask people for their opinions about how your church should respond to the environmental crisis in terms of the educate/evaluate/ exercise process. Ask them how they are responding in their own lifestyles and whether they have any skills or knowledge to contribute in this area. You may have a shy geomorphologist in your midst waiting to be asked! This information could be very valuable to leaders for their own planning, and build a strong base for local action.

• Consider the major environmental issues in your area. I am not just talking about a kind of NIMBY (not in my back yard) attitude which is only offended by ecological damage when it affects our own locality. But your area might have a cluttered-up stream, graffiti-strewn walls, or a factory belching toxic fumes. Can you take practical action (clean up the stream), political action (see the company directors) or both. At Revelation, we are writing to our MP about coastal pollution and cycleways, but we have held a mass litter collection as well.

• Consider making contact with your local MP. If your leaders have never met him or her, ask if a small group, including a leader, can meet them at one of their regular constituency surgeries. Politely indicate your concerns for the environment as a church, and raise any local issues of which you might be aware.

• Do you have a local group of the Movement for Christian Democracy? One of the six limbs of their Westminster Declaration is "wise stewardship", and the movement is committed to influencing the political structures. If there is a local MCD group why not join, or at least make contact and ask what they are doing on an environmental level. If there is not, start one! (See Appendix 2 for details).

• Take a questionnaire around the local shops and employers to find out about their environmental credentials. Write first asking for permission, and then ask about energy use, recycling, waste disposal, organic products, local products (saving energy), transport policies and so on. The local newspaper may be interested in publishing your results. Good fun, useful information and good profile for your church.

Notes

1 There has been a wide variety of opinion throughout church history right up to the present on how Jesus' teaching about the Kingdom should be interpreted. There are at least five different views, ranging from Kingdom as a synonym for the church, to a broad political idea that the Kingdom is present wherever righteousness, justice and love appear. Needless to say, I do not suggest that the interpretation I have adopted is in any way canonical. Appendix 2 suggests further reading.

2 Mark 4:30.

3 John 11:25.

4 Eg Luke 9:10.

5 Roger Forster lecture, *The Kingdom of God* at "Together for the Kingdom", Sheffield University, September 1988.

6 Matthew 6:10.

7 Attributed to Roger Forster.

8 I am grateful to Roger Ellis who allowed me to read his essay entitled, "The Gospel of the Kingdom". This forms part of the manuscript of his forthcoming book on church-planting which he is writing with Roger Mitchell.

9 Acts 1:8.
10 See Ephesians 1:13,14.
11 Eg see Matthew 7:28.
12 John 14:12.
13 Matthew 6:33.
14 See Matthew 5:6.
15 See Matthew 5:1–7:29.
16 See Philippians 2:12,13
17 See Luke 4:17–22.
18 Verse 19.
19 Sometimes known as the "parable of the prodigal son", this story is to be found in Luke 15:11–32.
20 2 Corinthians 5:19.
21 Verse 18.
22 Ephesians 2:14.
23 Naturally, world mission must remain as one of the Church's top priorities.
24 Matthew 28:19.
25 Matthew 19:28. The Greek word *palingenesia* means fresh and renewed, rather than new in time. It is interesting to note that this word is also used in Titus 3:5 of human spiritual rebirth, reinforcing the connection between the liberty God is bringing to people and to the whole creation.
26 Romans 14:7.
27 Vine, *ibid.*, p 852.
28 Matthew 16:19.
29 Matthew 18:18.
30 Howard Snyder *Liberating the Church*.
31 Ephesians 6:15.
32 These sheets, prepared for the *Whose Earth?* project, are available through *3rd Track* at Tear Fund.
33 I have drawn from the resources of the Christian Ecology Link in this section, particularly their papers *Christians and the Planet – How Green is the Church?* published in June 1990.
35 Quoted in Tim Cooper *Green Christianity* p 260.
36 *Ibid*.
37 The Sierra Club is a major environmental pressure group in the United States.
38 See Matthew 28:18.
39 S Bishop and C Droop *The Earth is the Lord's Regius* 1990, pp.56,57.
40 Ephesians 3:10.
41 Ephesians 6:11 (AV).
42 Incidently, I am eternally grateful to the Church of England for one of our local Sussex churchyards. Part of Pagham Harbour nature reserve, Church Norton offers refuge not only to annual avian visitors, but quite frequently to rare transatlantic and Eurasian vagrants as well.

Chapter 8

THE DAWNING OF A NEW GREEN AGE?

The Green Movement and New Age

Another Country

Spare a thought for Terry Waite and the other former Beirut hostages. When they left Britain it was a familiar Western nation; in the last five years everything has turned green! Supermarket chains, petrol companies and advertisers have been falling over one another to "green-up" their image and the image of their products. The environment is no longer a subject which is seen as a cure for insomnia in Parliament – every politician who wants to survive needs an active ecological conscience. Terry and the others could be forgiven for thinking they had returned to another country.

In this chapter I want to look at the broader influence of green issues which have had such a startling effect upon our culture recently. The so-called "green movement" is often talked about, but perhaps few people could accurately describe it. I want to consider not only what the green movement is but also how it compares with the Church – is it a threat? A mission field? Or a group from which we can learn and with whom we can find a measure of partnership? I then want to take a brief look at the New Age movement, which is often associated with all things green. Again there are a number of questions which need to be answered to help us gain the right understanding, and make a correct response to this trend.

Still in Vogue

Without a doubt, the Greens have made an astonishing achievement in putting the environment firmly on the nation's agenda. Everyone is aware of the need to take responsibility for our fragile planet home. For example, Prime Minister Major has picked up where his predecessor left off,

> "We must be global. We cannot wrap the environment up into neat, national parcels . . . What happens in Darlington or Detroit today may affect Dhaka or Djibouti tomorrow – and vice versa."[1]

It seems that the environment is not about to go out of fashion yet.

Remarkably this achievement does not owe its success to a carefully laid and centralised strategy, but rather to a potent grass-roots response to the ecological crisis. The use of the term "movement" suggests an organisational unity which simply does not exist as far as the Greens are concerned. On the level of structure, Friends of the Earth, Greenpeace, WWF and the Green Party share the same concerns and similar roots, but have considerable distinctives as well.

Historically, many of them share origins based around ideas contained in *Only One Earth*, written in 1972 by Barbara Ward and Rene Dubos, and the seminal economic work of EF Schumacher, *Small is Beautiful*. What has developed is a wide range of views whose supporters are variously described as deep ecologists, dark Greens, light Greens, shallow environmentalists, Green Socialists and even messianic ecologists!

In my opinion, the growth of green awareness has been one of the few signs of real hope, outside of Christ, in our society over recent years, and a genuine breath of fresh air. There are a number of clear parallels between the things that attract people to the Church and the things that attract people to the Green movement: a disillusionment with secular humanism and scientific materialism; a recognition of the need to recover a spiritual dimension in life; a vision of hope and a commitment to seek a change in the status quo. Naturally, there are some important distinctions as well, and I will touch upon these at the end of the chapter.

Towards a Definition of the Green Movement

However, for now it is worth setting out in a little more detail what lies at the heart of Green ideas. Drawing from the thoughts of a dark Green (Jonathon Porritt), a Christian Green (Tim Cooper), and the Green Party manifesto, I will add a few of my own comparisons with some biblical insights.

Biocentric

The centre of the Green philosophy is not humanity but the whole of the earth and its atmosphere: known scientifically as the "biosphere". This is why some Greens talk about "showing reverence" for the earth. It obviously brings with it beliefs about humankind's involvement with nature which would sit comfortably with the biblical paradigm of *shalom*, but less so with dominion and stewardship. Furthermore, the biblical world-view is clearly theocentric – God-centred, not earth-centred.

Holistic

Not only do Greens believe that the entire biosphere must be seen as central, but they emphasise the interconnectedness of all matter within it. Nothing can be viewed in isolation from anything else; everything must be integrated into the whole. This affects the methods which Greens adopt in their approach to every question: economics, health, education, sport or spirituality. It also explains why Greens have such little time for the scientific and technological approach which tends to view life as made up of separate and individual building blocks.[2]

Again, a truly biblical perspective on life must agree with this holistic attitude, but stress that connections exist because of the unity of creation as made by Almighty God, and because of the on-going presence of Christ who is holding all things together. Things are not simply interconnected just because we happen to be part of the same biosphere, but because of God's created order.

Radicalism

Rather than tinkering with the frills of society, or moving the deckchairs on the Titanic, the Green movement strives to go to the root of problems. Addressing materialism, consumerism, the power of corporations and of self-interest, Greens have not shied away from the tough questions. The Green Party manifesto describes the party as "a challenge to the established view of the nature of present social, political and economic system".[3]

The Bible affirms the importance of a radical approach. We shall see in the next chapter that it describes the love of money as "a root of all kinds of evil"[4] and of the radical nature of Jesus' coming Kingdom, another John said, "the axe is already laid to the root of the trees"[5]. In other words, the roots of the problems must be tackled, not just the fruit.

Sustainability

This recognises the rights of future generations to the use of all resources, and encourages development which will not compromise these rights. It refers not only to human sustainability but to all life. It is a motivating factor behind conservation and the protection of the environment, and is perhaps something which Greens of all shades would agree on.

A biblical perspective on sustainability must again clarify that it is Christ who sustains the planet and all its life. However, we bear a responsibility to act as his representatives and as the steward of his creation.

Decentralism

Opposing the tendency of both left-wing and right-wing politics towards centralised bureaucracy, the Green movement advocates self-reliance and decentralised communities. This includes an emphasis on open democracy in which everyone can truly get involved. Decentralism also touches on the issue of work – so many of us end up working to pay the bills and buy the food, to get the strength to be able to work, to pay the bills and buy the food . . . Work that is both socially useful and personally rewarding is surely worth more than the opposite, regardless of the pay-packet's size.

Naturally, with such a diverse philosophy there are many other features of Green thinking, including harmony between all peoples, non-violence and disarmament, an emphasis on the more gentle and reflective (or "feminine") aspects of humanity and a willingness to share out the world's resources more fairly among the world's population.

Here Come the Greens

So much for ideas. What are the issues that the Greens have raised over the past decade, and what have they done?

1. Environmental Action

The Greens are perhaps best known for their campaigning on behalf of environmental issues, and some astonishing results have been achieved. One of the leading pressure groups in the UK, with almost a quarter of a million supporters, Friends of the Earth, describe their role in this way,

> "We blow the whistle on those who destroy the environment, and put pressure on those who have the power to protect it."

Terrier-like in their pursuit of governments and businesses alike, FoE have had a significant influence on policy and legislation. They also offer expertise and educational resources and remain high-profile in the media.

Nevertheless, surely the greatest headline-grabbers are Greenpeace, well-known for steering their inflatable rafts between whaler's harpoons and their targets, bunging up radioactive-waste outlets into the Irish Sea and getting thrown into sub-zero temperature waters as they attempt to stop the clubbing of baby seals. Although they have seen tremendous successes, some supporters have paid the highest price. The most notable instance was the sinking of the Greenpeace flagship, *Rainbow Warrior*, in 1984 by the French secret services. One volunteer was killed in an admitted case of state-sponsored terrorism in Auckland Harbour, New Zealand.

Criticised by some as fanatics, Greenpeace have put the policy of "direct action" firmly on the map of peaceful protest. By taking these highly media-friendly actions, the opponents of Greenpeace are forced to defend their position – which they are rarely able to do! This in turn has succeeded in bringing seemingly remote issues to the public's attention.

Such actions are to be seen in contrast with groups like the Animal Liberation Front, whose policies have often rejected the tenet of non-violence. The contamination of baby food and soft drinks with poison to expose the manufacturers' cruelty to animals is met with horror by those who have adopted a more "gently green" approach.

2. Conservation

Groups calling for the conservation of natural habitats and wildlife – which have grown both in number and membership in the past decade – are sometimes seen as the softer, or lighter end of the green spectrum. As a member of one such charity myself, The Royal Society for the Protection of Birds (RSPB), it is plain that some great work is being done, but that many underlying problems and assumptions can go unchallenged.

The theologian Richard Russell has argued that modern conservation is often rooted either in pagan and mystical ideas of a sacred nature (which we will look at later), or on the basis of nature's usefulness to humanity.[6] In the latter case, people are still firmly in the centre of the picture.

One sometimes has the sneakiest of suspicions with the RSPB that the preservation of species is motivated more by the pleasure its members get from birding, than by the fact of the birds' God-given right to exist. The case of the "protection" of game-birds by the shooting lobby is an even more extreme and ironic example.

Having said all this, conservation is about maintaining the diversity of life and the ecological balance. Conservation bodies like the RSPB, the World Wide Fund for Nature (WWF) and many others, large and small, have influenced decision-makers to prevent local species extinction, destructive development projects and other "grey" policies. There is not much wrong with that.

3. Making Connections

Partly because the media has been so quick to jump on the "green bandwagon", (which, of course, it created in the first place) public awareness has been raised significantly concerning the environment. I have frequently quoted one of the green credos in this book: think globally, act locally, respond personally. I make no apology for doing so; I find it inspiring.

The fact that on a daily basis many people are *beginning* to take some responsibility for the planet through their consumption, their waste-disposal and their thinking should be applauded. Would there be the same growing interest in the rainforest and in Third World issues if the lessons of making connections had not been learned?

4. Green Politics

Politics is a funny old game. To those of us who have been brought up with the general British assumptions about life and with a degree of comfortable conservatism, anything politically radical is treated with suspicious indifference at best – and raging hysteria at worst! For this reason, the Green Party in Britain seems to excite quite a lot of interest and reaction.

From the early days of the Green movement in the 1970s,

it has always had a political dimension, and this is seen in the activity of most environmental and conservation bodies. However, the rise of Green political parties in many Western democracies was a phenomenon of the 1980s.[7] In the UK, the Ecology Party changed its name to the Green Party in 1987 when it won 1.36% of the vote in the general election of that year.[8] By the time of the elections to the European parliament in May 1989, the Green share of the vote had risen to almost 10%. Although its popularity has since dropped back, it certainly achieved the objective of putting green issues firmly on the political agenda.

The Green Party manifesto reflects the ethos which I have already set out in this chapter, seeking to "develop and implement ecological policies". One of the criticisms of the Party has been that because it tends to be radical, it touches very personal issues of life (perhaps contrasting with the dualistic perception of a public realm versus a private realm). One particularly well-publicised policy has been on the question of population, where couples are encouraged to limit the number of children they produce.[9] However, in response to claims of "ecofascism", the Green Party insists that "birth control would be encouraged by education – not by threat of sanctions."[10]

I am sometimes asked whether I believe a Christian can vote for the Green Party. The start of an answer to such a question must be that no political party (or Christian denomination or group for that matter) has a monopoly on the truth. Rather than looking at bits of policy here and there, the first thing to consider is the underlying aims and goals of a party; whether that be the individualistic capitalism of the Conservatives, the watered-down socialism of Labour, the uneasy mix of the centre parties or the radical environmentalism of the Greens.

In reality, most of us vote from a position of self-interest, but few of us would be "better off" by voting Green! True, there are a number of holes in the Green Party manifesto, (for example, its overall economic rationale is far from convincing) but its fundamental rejection of materialism, militarism and macho-politics will appeal to many Christians. Practically, one of the greatest weaknesses of our political structure is the "first past the post" voting system. This means that minority parties are unlikely to win many seats and therefore cannot exert their influence in Parliament. Unless you are in a marginal seat in a general election there is perhaps little incentive to vote Green even if you wanted to. However, the 1989 Green vote certainly woke the other parties up to the ecological debate so votes may not be wasted.

5. Vegetarianism

If ever there was a slogan to draw a response from people, to fire the emotions of supporters and to inflame the anger of opponents, the vegetarian cry of "meat is murder" must be it. To say that vegetarianism is quite a controversial issue, both within and outside the church, is like saying Mother Teresa is a nice old lady. The rising number of those who are turning to a vegetarian, or a more vegetarian[11] diet has reflected the fact that this is seen as a major environmental issue.

It is one thing to agree with green ideas of conservation and environmental awareness. It is one thing to accept a "greener theology". It is one thing even to go out of your way and act responsibly by recycling resources and being careful with your purchases. But it is quite another when it comes to our diet!

Somehow to our Western minds (or perhaps more accurately to our British minds) there is still a sensitivity about people telling us what we should and should not eat. Perhaps the chequered history of the politician, Edwina Currie, reflects this. We might be faced with an encyclopedia of facts and evidence about saturated fats causing health problems, but we do not like to be told to cut down on our fish and chips! We might be told that sugar will do nothing for our bodies except make us fat and rot our teeth, but most of us still like to heap it into our tea or shovel it onto our cornflakes.

As Christians we are used to working out priorities in life, understanding that just because we like to do something does not mean it is helpful for us – " 'Everything is permissible' – but not everything is beneficial" as Paul says.[12] So why is this practice such a struggle when it comes to our tums? Perhaps we are back to the different worldviews again – kidding ourselves into thinking that food is not a "spiritual" matter; not something that God is too bothered about. Certainly the writer of Proverbs has something strong to say about eating,

> "When you sit to dine with a ruler, note well what is before you, and put a knife to your throat if you are given to gluttony".[13]

Paul also touched on this subject when he described the enemies of the cross of Christ, "Their destiny is destruction, their god is their stomach, and their glory is in their shame".[14]

You might now be wondering if I am building up to tell you what *you* must and must not eat! Fear not but read on. The green agenda causes us to look at more than just vegetarianism, but at the whole area of animal welfare. The phrase "animal rights", like so many other buzz words with which we have learned to live, has put the question of the value of nature firmly to the fore of our consciousness. I said earlier that vegetarianism is a matter of great controversy, but the wider problem of the morality of our involvement with animals seems to raise people's temperature no less.

There are clearly some aspects of the way in which we treat animals in Britain which reflect double standards. We all like to watch the Davids Attenborough and Bellamy taking us through their wildlife broadcasts to show us the wonders of animal life. Many find a unique companionship through a pet dog or budgie and as a nation we give millions of pounds to animal charities such as the RSPCA and PDSA.

Yet each year thousands of these pets are thrown into the streets and end up as strays, bloodsports are still popular and the cruel conditions in most slaughterhouses to put meat on our table are such that, according to one writer, "if the walls were made of glass we would all be vegetarian".[15] Chicken-farming often throws up the most disturbing of accounts,

> "At one day old the chicks are taken out of the incubator and sexed – which means separating the males from the females. Of course there is no future for the males, so these are either gassed, drowned or crushed in metal tubs or containers. In some cases the dead chicks are recycled into animal feed or dumped on tips. I have seen chicks which have not been properly killed left to die in agony for hours . . ."[16]

The rest of the article gets worse. It is in this context that people turn not only *off* meat-eating, but in some cases *towards* violence on behalf of animals.

Another worrying dimension to factory farming is that of genetic engineering. To enhance productivity and hence profit, new types of animals are being "created" in the laboratory, with who knows what results. There are currently attempts to allow scientists to have "creator's rights" and to patent their animal creations. Quite apart from the general health concerns of such experimentation, there are grave ethical and biblical problems. It has been observed that this disobeys the laws of order given to the Israelites ("Do not mate different kinds of animals"[17]) and reminds one of Isaiah's words against the king of Babylon,

> I will make myself like the Most High.[18]

Apart from all the issues of cruelty to animals themselves – vivisection, factory farming, and so on – and the wider concerns of genetic engineering, there is another question which needs to be faced to gain a wholistic view on the matter. That is the question of grain-fed beef. On the menu, food is food and it makes little difference what we choose to eat. But how many people realise that a huge proportion of UK grain consumption goes to producing meat? In fact, it takes thirteen pounds of grain for a fattening cow to put on one pound of edible meat.[19] The developed countries use more grain for livestock than the developing countries use for livestock *and* eat directly – even though their populations are two-thirds larger! It is partly because of this high level of meat consumption that the rich minority of the world eats an unfair proportion of the world's food.

How do we find our way through these complexities and where should Christians stand on this controversy? Certainly, in the context of *shalom*, a biblical attitude to animals must neither be based on mere usefulness nor allow unnecessary cruelty. It would seem that humanity was vegetarian before the fall[20] and that meat-eating was only specifically permitted after the flood.[21] It has also been argued from the prophetic visions, particularly of Isaiah, that people will again be vegetarian in the fulness of the Kingdom.[22] A close relationship between humanity and animals is affirmed by Scripture: Adam named the animals,[23] sharing in his Maker's care for the welfare of his creation; God made the covenant of the rainbow with Noah and "with every living creature with you";[24] and the blood of the Passover was effective for Israel *and* for their animals.[25]

On the other hand, Jesus did eat fish[26] and as a ceremonially-correct Jew would have probably eaten animal sacrifices. Neither he nor any of his followers are described as vegetarians in the Gospels, and the New Testament makes it clear that nothing is to be considered unclean "if it is received with thanksgiving".[27] The vegetarian Christian must beware of a kind of gnostic[28] attitude which suggests that they have acquired a superior, enlightened form of faith – this is not supported biblically.

Other Christians have taken a very negative view of

vegetarianism due to what I believe is a misinterpretation of Romans 14:2,

> "One man's faith allows him to eat everything, but another man, whose faith is weak, eats only vegetables."

This has been taken by some to mean that a vegetarian has a weaker faith than a meat-eater. However, Paul is not entering the debate on the same basis of ethics as we would discuss it today. The context was a pagan culture in which meat was ceremonially offered to idols before being sold in the market – the person of weak faith did not recognise that Christ's sacrifice had destroyed both the food laws, and the power of Satan over such rituals. It had little to do with sharing the world's resources or concern about cruelty to animals.

Ironically, the message of Romans 14 advocates the opposite to the kind of strident attitude with which vegetarians are sometimes condemned, "*Accept* him whose faith is weak . . . The man who eats everything *must not* look down on him who does not."[29] (Italics mine.)

Given all of this, vegetarianism must be an option for the believer, and should be seriously considered especially in the light of factory farming, brutal slaughterhouses and sometimes vicious laboratory experiments. Further, if we are to be responsible planetary citizens, we must recognise that our meat-eating is contributing to the imbalance of the global diet.

On the other hand, once you start on the road to non-exploitation of animals, it is hard to know where to stop – vegetarian, vegan, no leather, no honey, where next? It seems to be a bit of an ethical skidpan to me. Of course, this does not mean that we should "use [our] freedom as a cover-up for evil."[30] Hunting, shooting and other bloodthirsty pastimes appear to be quite inconsistent with a non-violent gospel of peace.

Perhaps the issue for Christians as far as meat-eating is concerned, is not necessarily vegetarianism as such, but more in line with choosing between factory-farming or free-range production. Whilst the latter costs more, buying free-range avoids the cruel excesses of factory-farming and the reservations about genetic engineering. It is also more ethical consumerism in the light of Third World poverty.

In summary, "the Kingdom of God is not a matter of eating and drinking, but of righteousness, peace and joy in the Holy Spirit,"[31] but as with all things we have a duty to live as stewards of God's creation and at *shalom* with nature. We cannot divorce our eating, or any aspect of our lifestyle, from our faith if we are "offering our bodies as living sacrifices, holy and pleasing to God."[32]

6. Holistic Spirituality

The final issue which the Green movement has raised over the past two decades is what is vaguely termed "spirituality". Rejecting humanism and seeking a sense of wholeness and harmony with the earth has caused Greens to look around for something far more deep and "holistic" than the mechanical, materialistic ways of Western cultures. Indeed, it seems that to embrace a green view of life inevitably involves some form of spiritual expression or commitment. The precise form that this expression takes does not seem to be too important and it is rather unlikely that any single religion could monopolise the movement. This is reflected in an editorial of one of the major North American green periodicals,

> "What you call yourself is not relevant. Christian, Muslim, Buddhist, Hindu, Jew, Druid, Jain, Shaman or any of the World's diverse and varied faiths. The name is unimportant. What is important is the recognition that God is Love and that Love is Passion and it is Passion that directs us, inflames us, controls us and provides the strength to really make a difference in the World."[33]

Both because it is exclusive and because it is usually associated – fairly or unfairly – with Western technological cultures, Christianity has rarely been a "first stop" on the spiritual pilgrimage of an uncommitted Green. Instead, people have drawn upon a number of oriental religions and philosophies including Taoism, Zen Buddhism, Hinduism and animistic religions like Shamanism. These are often described under the banner of "new consciousness" or more popularly, "New Age".

Due both to its complexity and to lack of space here, I do not propose to discuss the New Age movement (NAM) at the fullest length it deserves. Appendix 2 includes a number of excellent, balanced works on the NAM from which more information can be gleaned. I would simply like to provide some background to New Age ideas, point to their dangers, comment on the Christian reaction so far and suggest a positive response.

Fresh Enlightenment . . .

One of the things that is clear about the NAM is that its name is highly misleading – it is neither new nor a clearly defined movement! If the green movement is diverse and eclectic, then the NAM is a bewildering array of scientific, pyschological, sociological and spiritual ideas. It has gained a dominant position in the mindset of many people who live in the West Coast area of North America, and is gradually spreading east to influence other parts of the USA and Europe. Whilst there is a tendency for those sharing a similar outlook on life to want to "network" together on the basis of holistic health or similar common interests, I want to say that I can see no centralised strategy or organisation within the NAM. I do not believe in the conspiracy theory as such, although there is certainly a common desire to achieve a "paradigm shift".

Shifting Paradigms

The phrase "New Age" comes from one of the central tenets of NAM thinking, which holds that humanity is on the brink of a "new age" of knowing. In other words, it is stated that a new kind of science is emerging which will change the way in which we interpret knowledge. This concept is highly dependent on the ideas of Thomas Kuhn, an historian and philosopher of science, who wrote *The Structure of Scientific Revolutions*.[34] Kuhn states that the way in which science develops is not through additions to a body of knowledge, but through "paradigm shifts". That is, by changes in the "windows" of interpretation which are used.

Paradigm shifts are important. For example, in Part Two of this book I have suggested a paradigm shift is required in our approach to humanity's relations with nature. The window of "dominion" as domination is less helpful than the window of *shalom*. When a number of anomalies can be seen in the way in which a subject is interpreted, the framework for that interpretation probably needs to be shifted.

The most common illustration of such a shift from the world of science is found in what is known as "the Copernican Revolution" which culminated in the seventeenth century.[35] This describes how the earth-centred model of the heavens was replaced by a sun-centred model, reaching its climax around the time of the trial of Galileo. Indirectly, this paradigm shift is said to have inspired many of the "new" ideas of influential thinkers like Descartes, Newton and Bacon. In turn, these ideas of the Enlightenment are said to have enabled so much damage to be wreaked upon the global environment and the human psyche alike.

Recently discovered scientific phenomena such as holograms and quarks (described as "patterns of loving energy",[36]) the claimed abolition of the second law of thermodynamics and the Einstein-Podolsky-Rosen experiment are quoted in New Age writings to show the need for another paradigm shift.[37] It is suggested that a change on the scale of the Reformation or the Renaissance will be required to embrace this new knowledge.

However, the NAM is by no means confined to the realm of science. Many writers (most notably Fritjof Capra and Marilyn Ferguson) have been quick to point out the spiritual implications of modern physics. The "New Age" is not only one of scientific knowledge, but more particularly about a change in spiritual awareness, represented by the astrological Age of Pisces giving way to the Age of Aquarius. The themes of unity, holism and interconnectedness are often taken to far extremes and the general conclusion reached is that we all need to find a higher consciousness as a part of the one cosmic energy. Awash in a sea of monism, the door is opened to a variety of occult, mystical and paranormal experiences.

Thin End of a Wedge

The monism of Eastern religions, popularised in the West during the 1960s partly by the Beatles' association with the Mahareshi Yogi and by their experimentation with TM, has made steady progress from its origins in the hippy, counter-culture. Meditation techniques, mood-altering music, special diets, holistic health products and psychotherapeutic programmes are advertised in most health food shops, magazines, and community centres. Behind the mask of modern and technical-sounding names like reflexology, aromatherapy and acupuncture lie a number of ancient, mystical and occultic ideas – hence my suggestion that the NAM is not that new. One author, Roger Ellis, has compared the presentation of New Age ideas with a "cover version" of an old song into a modern pop hit,

> " . . . no matter how much they speed up or slow down the song, and no matter how different the arrangement is, the tune remains the same. The stamp of the original writer is still there."[38]

Around the centre of the spectrum, some New Age ideas are no more than a re-mix of Taoism, Buddhism and Hinduism. Whilst at the thicker end of the spiritual wedge, the pagan religions, Wicca, Shamanism and Druidism are a thin veil for the occult, and "mind-expanding" drug-taking is sometimes encouraged.[39]

The NAM has been criticised for being a bit of a comfortable middle-class trend – the materialism and hedonism (or pursuit of pleasure) in our culture apparently go quite unthreatened. New Agers seem to have a near-obsession with "self", emphasising self-development, self-healing and self-discovery. The goal is to achieve "self-realisation", based on the belief that people have virtually unlimited potential which is largely unfulfilled. This in turn will lead to a kind of global consciousness in which we all become like "God", that is, find our identity in the one ultimate reality. This idea has been popularised by the statements of actress Shirley Maclaine that "I am God" and of David Spangler that "we are each our own Christ".

Meet Gaia

As we have seen, much of the New Age thinking tends to be a kind of mish-mash of science and religion. The Gaia hypothesis, proposed by James Lovelock and Lynn Margulis, is an example which is particularly relevant to the Green debate.[40] The hypothesis is supported by biological and physical facts which have been uncovered to show that the delicate balance of gases, the flow of nutrients and the other cycles of life represent far more than the operation of individual organisms. "Something" seems to be monitoring and controlling these elements – a fascinating and inspiring suggestion.

However, the interpretation of this information by Lovelock and his friends is both novel and controversial. They argue that the whole earth is itself a huge, single organism, with its own intelligence, and of which we are only a part. Further, this organism has been named "Gaia", after the Greek earth goddess. Evoking the pagan ideas of "Mother Earth", Lovelock believes that,

> "Gaia [will] reward mankind with her bounty when treated well, but equally she [will] revenge abuse."[41]

. . . or Devilish Conspiracy?

Given my own position as neither a very dark nor a very light Green Christian (as a meat-eating Green, perhaps "medium rare" would be closest!), I must confess to feeling quite dismayed at the polarised response of the Church to the NAM. Of course, there are those who present a balanced and sensible perspective, but these voices are often drowned out by those from the extremes.

On the one hand, there are plainly a number of things about the NAM that should cause great concern from a biblical worldview. These can be summarised quite briefly.

Monism

Monism is a common thread throughout the spirituality of the NAM, spoken of as a kind of "cosmic energy" and "global consciousness". It is quite alien to the notion of God being both before and above everything[42] that he has created. As I mentioned in Chapter 6, the right sort of *dualism*, which distinguishes between Creator and creatures, and the separation (or *duality*) of God and Satan, are essential to our understanding of who God is.

Pantheism

Likewise, we must reject the idea that the earth itself is God. The Gaia hypothesis offers facts which I believe wonderfully support the biblical statement which I have referred to so frequently, that in Christ "all things hold together".[43] But, to use theological language, God is both *transcendant* (above and beyond), as well as *immanent* (indwelling and pervading) within creation. Gaia therefore presents a modern and sophisticated form of nature-religion, harking back to both paganism and to Romantics like Coleridge and Wordsworth.

There is also a particular dimension of Gaia which does not quite seem to add up. If humanity is really only part of this one giant, complex, planet-sized organism, why do we have the power and the apparent willingness to throw a spanner in the whole system with such disastrous results?

Occultism
The apostle Paul asks rhetorically,

> ". . . what fellowship can light have with darkness? What harmony is there between Christ and Belial?[44] . . . What agreement is there between the temple of God and idols?"[45]

No matter how stale our experience of organised Christianity might be, there is absolutely no room for compromise with the occult. The Bible is absolutely clear that mediumism, spiritism and astrology[46] are the works of a subtle and devious enemy and we mess with them at our peril.

Self-centred
Far from seeking to "realise" ourselves, the Bible exhorts us to take up our Cross and follow Christ.[47] This does not mean we accept the burden of being a Christian as some have suggested! Rather, it means that we willingly die to ourselves and live for Christ and his Kingdom. This is why Paul says, "I no longer live, but Christ lives in me".[48]

Salvation
Vague notions of the potential in all people, and the need to acquire "global consciousness" do not square with the Bible's view of salvation. The issue of sin is ducked in the NAM (as in most Eastern religions), and the Christian distinctive of Jesus' atoning sacrifice has no place in its worldview.

Eschatology or "End Times"
A Christian seeks *communion* with God and ultimately a fulfilled relationship with him in a coming Kingdom, but not *union* with God – an absorption into the one true reality. The New Agers do not really believe in "the end times" as their view of life would be more cyclical (hence the popularity of reincarnation in NAM thought). However,

they do have a goal, which is a kind of global oneness, bringing in the Aquarian qualities of peace, harmony and unity. The reality of peace without the personal God of creation is meaningless from a biblical perspective. As the prophet observed, " 'Peace, peace,' they say, when there is no peace."[49]

Again, it is the denial of personal sin and of the need for personal forgiveness, salvation and cleansing offered by Christ which separates NAM thought from reality as presented in the Scriptures.

Uneasy Bedfellows

From all that I have just stated it becomes apparent that biblical Christianity and the NAM are fundamentally different on a number of counts. This is why it is disturbing that there appears to be such a high tolerance of New Age and non-biblical ideas among green Christians. Of course, our approach to all humanity must be loving, to all perspectives respectful and to all those with whom we disagree, gracious. However, in entering into conversation with New Agers we must be absolutely sure of who and what we are in Christ. I am not talking about "simply repeating the formulae of our religion, bludgeoning anyone we can get to listen with our pre-worked out answers to our own pre-set questions",[50] as has been suggested.

Instead, I am talking about a Christ-centred view of creation and of green issues. Sadly, because evangelicals in particular have been so slow to involve themselves in thinking about the earth, and in talking to Greens, the green *Christian* movement looks more like a Christian *green* movement. Many of its supporters hail from groups and denominations which seem to hold the Bible no higher than tradition – the words of Paul of Tarsus are no more valuable than those of Francis of Assisi. It appears that some Christians are trying to fit their faith into their green awareness rather than vice versa.

Certainly, we need vigorous involvement and engagement in these issues from every part of the Church. Orthodox,

Catholic and Anglican traditions certainly have a vital role in helping us to think through some tough questions which we face in seeking to "green the Church". However, perhaps we have less to thank the liberal theologians for. Unless our doctrinal roots are secure in a firm Christological view of the Bible we will surely find ourselves on a hermeneutical skidpan, unable to interpret it properly. This means we can more easily fall prey to New Age explanations of truth.

The apostle John, who had to deal with many heresies in his ministry, said this,

> "Anyone who runs ahead and does not continue in the teaching [AV = doctrine] of Christ does not have God; whoever continues in the teaching has both the Father and the Son."[51]

For many Christians talk about a search for the "cosmic Christ", developing a Global Spirituality and exploring the "God Within" (all ideas, events and articles advertised in CEL's *Green Christians*) will be seen as "running ahead" of orthodox biblical doctrine. These novel theological ideas, which undoubtedly owe their inspiration to New Age influences, raise real concerns about the place of Christ in so-called green Christianity. Certainly, I regret that they put me seriously at odds with many fellow Christians who want to see a greener gospel. Sadly, these concerns were only reinforced by the choice of one of the main speakers to the 1991 CEL conference, a Roman Catholic priest whose teaching was regarded by many as mainstream New Age!

Greens under the Bed?

Frustrating as this situation is, the other "pole" of reaction to the NAM is positively infuriating! Having said that the dangers of New Age thought need to be exposed, some books which have been written on the subject read more like a conspiracy-hunt[52] than an exposé. Two or three works in particular, almost a decade old now, have cast a long shadow over the whole subject of the NAM. They have contributed to a near-hysterical response in some parts of the evangelical church.

Whilst the authors do raise very proper concerns, they unfortunately discount a great deal of the science which lies behind the ecological and pyschological elements of the NAM. Greatly exaggerating the level of occult activity in the NAM, they claim that all the talk of a more fair world order, ecological responsibility and the need to redistribute the world's resources is a cunning Satanic plan. Worse, they suggest that all attempts at environmental stewardship are part of the same plot, including any use of words like "holistic", "ecological" or "global village".

Worse still, any Christian author or speaker who writes or preaches on these themes, or uses the defiled vocabulary, is guilty by assocation. In this way, such giants of American christendom as Ronald Sider, Tom Sine, Jim Wallis and John Wimber have been condemned. There seems something quite distressing, if not outright immoral, about suggesting that all Christians who are calling for a redistribution of the world's wealth on behalf of the poorest and most oppressed nations, are really a part of a huge demonic game-plan!

Holding the Tension

According to Dave Tomlinson, the result of this view being accepted at large has been that the NAM has taken over as the Church's "new demon" after the demise of its former pet enemy, communism.[53] However, we should all welcome teaching that helps us sort out what Satan is doing in the world. The NAM does present a real threat to the truth: it offers people a "map and compass" to understand life which competes with the Christian faith in important ways. It is also one which is based on selfishness and on a dubious moral framework. Finally it does often encourage demonic principles and practices and has led many people into spiritual bondage.

But let's keep some balance. First, the impact of New Age influence on the work of the Church should be examined carefully. Is it really more significant and destructive than say materialism, dead religion, or gossip? The enemies within are always the most dangerous. Second, some New Agers consider Christians to be part of the NAM! After all, most of us begin our journey from some degree of disillusionment with what materialism and humanism can offer. We are all looking for God, and Christians have found their Christ. Third, the NAM does have some good ideas. For example, the understanding of interconnectedness in the earth, the strong ecological ethic (which of course attracts so many Greens) and some of the scientific interpretations are rather difficult to argue against.

"Take this 'plane to Nirvana"

To summarise the NAM, it has been described in perhaps its most balanced way by Russell Chandler who says it is, "neither the hellish conspiracy that fundamentalist critics charge, nor the utopian bliss its fondest supporters imagine."[54] There are some positives. For example, do not the New Age interpretations of science offer a provocation to Christians to think about the theology of modern physics? There should be no threat about challenges laid at some of our most cherished assumptions.

However, the NAM has (quite successfully) attempted to hi-jack the whole green agenda. Hi-jackers take control of an aircraft and force it to be flown to their desired destination. As far as the Bible is concerned, "the earth is the Lord's and everything in it."[55] That is the direction of thinking that the Church is called to proclaim. But our voice has been too quiet in the cultural market-place of ideas and the loudest has been "Mother Earth is us, and we must all take care of her"! A new direction has been taken; the initiative has been lost.

Unfortunately, due to the fundamentalist knee-jerking of a few, I fear that the Church may have shot itself in the proverbial foot in terms of reaching many Greens and New Agers with the Gospel. However, I do not believe that the battle is lost. The Green movement does not have a clear spiritual framework, and perhaps never will have. This means it is not beyond redemption and that now is the time for the Church to put the metaphorical aeroplane back on course.

Conclusion

By way of concluding this brief look at the Green movement, I would like to emphasise some of its main distinctions from the Christian faith.

The greatest of these distinctions is that whilst Christianity is a *faith* or "ultimate commitment"[56] Green ideas are a *philosophy*, based on a framework of thought. People in the Green movement may hold a variety of different spiritual worldviews which underlie their Green awareness. Perhaps because of their passion and commitment to a different framework of ideas from other "secular" groups, it has sometimes been assumed that Greens have invented a new religion based around reverence for the earth. Clearly, for many people who are discovering ecology and a more wholistic way of life, a greater awareness of their spiritual hunger becomes apparent. Partly for the reasons suggested in Chapter 6 and outlined above, the Christian faith has seemed a poor option to many Greens; New Age and Eastern faiths have often appeared to be more attractive.

In saying this, even without the Green/New Age overlap, a note of caution must be raised about the "green goal". A Christian's concern for the planet is not centred around the earth itself, but around Christ. For Jesus was, "In the beginning . . . with God",[57] and he will forever be,

> ". . . the radiance of God's glory and the exact representation of his being, sustaining all things by his powerful word."[58]

For this reason, the Church is not on a mission to "save the planet" – this is well out of our league! The theological perspective of creation, fall and redemption reveals that God alone has the power to "renew all things".[59] Only in him are we able to find true wholeness, and thereby wholeness with and within the creation. This is why I believe that the gospel of the Kingdom is good news indeed to Greens who are struggling under the weight of responsibility and the conflict of "fighting back" for the earth, whilst conscious of a lack of real inner peace.

Having said this, it should mean that much of a Christian environmental ethic will overlap with what the Greens are doing. But our motivation and assumptions will always remain quite distinct.

The overall challenge is surely, "how should the Church respond to the Green movement?" To address my questions at the start of this chapter, first I do not believe that the Green movement is a threat to Christianity. As a philosophy, a Christian can (and should?) embrace many of its ideas within a biblical framework. The New Age movement is a different kettle of fish as we have now seen!

Second, I do not believe it wrong to consider the Green movement a mission field, for the reasons stated above. What could be more wholistic than being reconciled to one's Maker? Further, is it beyond belief that the impact of the Green movement in Britain, with its rejection of some of the idols of our time, and its spiritual emphasis, could be used by God to "pre-evangelise" many people? I believe not.

Finally, I think we can learn from the Green movement and must be humble enough to admit it. As Wilkinson has observed,[60] whilst the Church tries to develop an environmental ethic we are not setting, but following, a general cultural trend. If we resign ourselves to the fact that the Green movement is beyond redemption, the New Age hi-jack succeeds for certain. If we can get involved with green and environmental initiatives we begin to contest this hi-jack. It might commit us to partnership from time to time with non-Christian green groups. This should not cause us too much concern as our mandate for involvement in society, found in Matthew 5:17–19, means that if we are salty and full of flavour, we will make a difference.

The Lausanne Covenant wrote of "co-belligerence" or fighting on issues with others. I do not have to agree with everything that David Alton believes to fight with him on the life issue. Neither do I have to become like David Icke, or agree with every word of Mr Porritt to vote Green or join Friends of the Earth!

Participation and a commitment to action are the only ways forward. We cannot turn the clock back – if we could, we might be leading the Green movement as we have been given grace to do in some other areas recently.[61] A lack of involvement could be perilous. I am reminded of the parable of the sheep and goats, when the people in front of the judgement throne ask of Jesus the question, "when did we see you?". His reply showed that connections should have been made.[62]

Practical Steps

Thinking about the issues of the New Age, the Green movement and vegetarianism is not enough. Below I have set out a few ways of dipping your toes into these murky waters! For further details look under the relevant sections of Appendix 2.

- Get yourself clued up on the NAM. Read something sensible on the subject like *The New Age and You* by Andrea Clarke and Roger Ellis, or one of the other books recommended in Appendix 2. A proper understanding of the NAM will help you to explain it to others and give you the confidence to mix with Greens without becoming deceived, and without fear of getting "contaminated" by New Age ideas.
- Consider joining one of the national environmental groups. Contrary to popular belief, many of them are really quite sane and their information gathering on green issues is second to none. I am a member of Friends of the Earth, which is primarily a political and social pressure group.

I would have some reservations about joining Greenpeace, which admit to being born out of their founders' experience in Shamanism (a North American form of animism).[63]

- Look in your local paper (or in a local health food shop!) for details of Green groups which meet near you. Alternatively contact the national headquarters of any of the better-known organisations and ask them what they are doing in your area. Why not go along to one or two, find out what they are about, and about the issues of concern in your area?
- The benefits of active participation are that you get involved in green issues at the sharp end, and you will also make contact with those outside the Church who share your concern for the earth. The reason for your interest in Green issues is bound to be a good conversation starter! A third benefit will be that you can make your own mind up about New Age infiltration in your area.
- If you get involved in an environmental group, do keep your friends and your church leaders informed about what is going on. Encourage your church to pray (i) about the environmental issues, (ii) for those in the groups, (iii) for your protection. In the past, active green Christians have too often ended up marginalised and frustrated, with their faith shipwrecked. This has usually been due to lack of church understanding and support, and because of some individuals' imbalanced priorities. Remember, if Satan can't stop you he will try to push you over the top!
- Write to the Vegetarian Society or CEL and ask for information about vegetarianism. It is not enough to avoid the ethical questions about meat-eating: the final choice you make is less important than having sought God with open heart. If you are "veggie", or "non-veggie", because of peer pressure, prejudice or as a hangover from New Age or occult involvement in the past, then it is unlikely that your decision has been made in faith. "And without faith, it is impossible to please God . . ."[64]
- If you do continue to eat meat, you could cut down on the amount of red and white meat in your diet. Apart

from the good health grounds, which I have not gone into in this chapter, it will have a direct impact on the amount of the world's food resources we consume. Also, try and find a supplier of meat which has been reared and killed with minimum cruelty. This will rule out supermarkets and most of the major chains of butchers. A combination of these approaches has been adopted by our family.

Notes

1 Quoted in *Earth Matters*, Autumn 1991.
2 This approach is broadly described as "reductionism".
3 Green Party *Manifesto for a Sustainable Society* 1990 PB103.
4 1 Timothy 6:10.
5 Matthew 3:10.
6 See his excellent paper, *Creation and Conservation*, copies of which are available from the Christian Studies Unit (Appendix 2 for address).
7 The first green party (known as the Values Party) was founded in New Zealand in 1972, but it was to the Bundestag in West Germany in 1983 that the first Green politicians were elected.
8 Goldsmith and Hildyard *The Earth Report* Mitchell Beazley 1988 p 157.
9 Eg "There should be an increase in 'only' children." The Green Party *ibid.* p506.
10 Telephone conversation with Green Party spokesman, 21 November, 1991.
11 In 1984 4% of the UK population avoided all red meat and white meat or were vegetarian or vegan. By 1988 this figure was 8.5%. (Gallup).
12 1 Corinthians 10:23.
13 Proverbs 23:1,2.
14 Philippians 3:19.
15 Quoted in Christian Ecology Link leaflet, *Some Thoughts on Vegetarianism*.
16 Brian Mills, *Animal Christian Concern News*, Summer 1990.
17 Leviticus 19:19.
18 Isaiah 14:14b.
19 Sider *Rich Christians in an Age of Hunger* IVP 1977, p 36.
20 See Genesis 1:29.
21 See Genesis 9:3.
22 See Russell, *ibid.*
23 Genesis 2:19.
24 Genesis 9:12.
25 Exodus 11:4–7.

26 Matthew 14:17–20; Luke 24:42,43.
27 1 Timothy 4:4. See also Romans 14:14 and Acts 10:9–21.
28 See Appendix 1.
29 Romans 14:1,3.
30 1 Peter 2:16.
31 Romans 14:17.
32 Romans 12:1.
33 Captain Paul Watson, "The Ecology of Spirit", *Sea Shepherd Log* Spring 1991.
34 University of Chicago Press, 1962.
35 See Loren Wilkinson's essay, "New Age, New Consciousness, and the New Creation" in *Tending the Garden* Eerdmans, 1987, pp 12,13.
36 Diarmuid O'Murchu, lecture on *Health and Salvation*, CEL Conference, Cliff College, July 1991.
37 Wilkinson, *ibid.*, pp 10–18.
38 *The Occult and Young People* Kingsway, 1989, pp 80,81.
39 Eg Available book titles include *The Wondrous Mushroom* and *LSD: The Age of Mind.*
40 See Lovelock's *Gaia: A New Look at Life on Earth* OUP, 1979.
41 "Man and Gaia" in *The Earth Report*, *ibid.* p 64.
42 Colossians 1:15; Ephesians 1:21.
43 Colossians 1:17.
44 "Belial", like "Beelzebub", is a Greek word sometimes used as a proper name for Satan. In this passage it represents "a personification of the system of impure worship connected especially with the cult of Aphrodite." (Vine, ibid., p 118).
45 2 Corinthians 6:15,16.
46 Eg Deuteronomy 18:9–13; Isaiah 47:13–15.
47 Luke 9:23.
48 Galatians 2:20.
49 Jeremiah 8:11.
50 Peter Cox, Editorial Comment in *Green Christians* (the CEL Newsletter), November 1991 – January 1992.
51 2 John 9.
52 Wilkinson describes conspiracy-hunting as, "that time-honored element of American fundamentalism", *ibid.*, p24.
53 *Green Christianity* lecture, ibid.
54 Russell Chandler *Understanding the New Age* Word, 1988, p.18.
55 Psalm 24:1.
56 I prefer these terms to the phrase "religion" which suggests rigid organisational structure, ritual and a system – none of which are found in the New Testament.
57 John 1:1,2.
58 Hebrews 1:3.
59 Matthew 19:28.

60 *Ibid.*, p 7.
61 I am thinking particularly of the work of ACET, the Christian HIV and Aids charity.
62 Matthew 25:31–46.
63 See "Animism" in Appendix 1.
64 Hebrews 11:6.

Chapter 9

TALKIN' 'BOUT MONEY

Making Connections

"The best things in life are free," goes the old proverb. "But you can give them to the birds and the bees, 'cos I want money – that's what I want!" This is how the old blues number humorously picks up the theme, showing that when it comes down to value in our culture we're talking Money with a capital "M". Whether simply the latest chocolate bar or the hottest fuel-injected hatchback its all about dosh. The size of your wad determines whether you measure up with the latest 501s or make do with a more modest pair of jeans without a television-advertised label. The message is clear, without the readies, you're nothing.

The song *Money* is one of many popular anthems[1] which have been written exposing the often mindless pursuit of spondulix which is such a feature of our society. Of all the practical questions which need to be faced from a green perspective of God's world, finance is right at the top of my list. Whilst it is easy to feel guilty when we look at subjects like this, we must remember that God does not want us to be motivated by guilt. All he asks for is a mind willing to be changed, and a heart open to his voice. As Jesus said, "He who has ears, let him hear."[2]

As a Christian, one of the debts I believe the Church owes to the Green Movement is the lesson of making connections. To think globally, act locally and respond personally is such an appropriate message for the 1990s, but it is the timeless message of the Bible. A shame the Greens had to remind us of this!

When it comes to money the reality is stunningly simple: what you and I do with the pound in our pocket either reinforces the status quo or speaks prophetically of something altogether different. A biblical approach to personal finance is not just about being honest (that surely goes without saying!) but about declaring the Kingdom in a very tangible way.

Another example that Greens have set the Church is the determination to translate a set of beliefs about economics into a radical lifestyle. Some of the methods used and some of the end results may not be to our liking but as I suggested in the last chapter, it might only be our conservatism that is being offended. I have repeated frequently that the historic dualism and hypocrisy of saying we believe one thing about such issues as money, and yet live out another has been a plague on the Church for too long.

To be true radicals, Christians must face the challenge of a root and branches review of how we handle our monies, individual and corporate. To be agents of the Kingdom will require us to have a lifestyle which is very distinct from that around us. In a materialistic age – and one that is wearing thin – I am sure that a liberating attitude to finance is something that many people secretly yearn for.

Money Makes The World Go Around

Before returning to our personal response, it is important to look at the global picture. Put crudely, the world is most easily divided between those who are and those who are not "holding folding". The distinctions are described variously as First World/Third World (now seriously out of fashion),[3] developed/developing,[4] North/South (popularised by the 1980 Brandt Report)[5] or more simply as rich/poor. In her excellent and inspiring book, *A Fate Worse Than Debt*, Susan George says that the most accurate description of all would also be the bluntest – "dominating" and "dominated".[6]

Britain is fairly typical of a "North" culture where the appetite for more and more material wealth, and the desire to consume seem to be insatiable. To look beneath the surface, it seems quite plain that there are a number of roots to the problems of wealth and poverty; of starvation and excess. The primary causes must surely be described in spiritual terms. I would like to describe two of these roots: one being spiritual hunger, and the other idolatry.

1. Spiritual Hunger

Detached from relationship with God as a result of sin, humanity is incapable of totally insulating itself from spiritual hunger. Once the basics of life have been met and we are free from starvation, thirst, cold, physical threat and so on, there are always new needs that await satisfaction. Expressed plainly, material consumption attempts to fill the spiritual vacuum created by a lack of purpose and security at a deeper level.

Of all people, Mother Teresa is the last one would expect to read making the following statement,

> "The biggest disease today is not leprosy or tuberculosis, but the feeling of being unwanted, uncared for and deserted by everybody. Our greatest problem is not hunger but loneliness."[7]

This spiritual and emotional famine knows no economic boundaries, and was observed by one of the pioneers of the German Green movement when he moved from what was East to West Germany,

> "There has never been so much unhappiness as there is in the rich countries today – anxiety, discontent, loneliness either with or without other people, failure and alienation of every kind – not even in the darkest and most impoverished of times."[8]

Only Jesus can truly quench this hungering and thirsting. In his dialogue with the woman at the well, he described the living water of his *zoe* life,

> "Everyone who drinks this water will be thirsty again, but whoever drinks the water I give him will never thirst. Indeed, the water I give will become in him a spring of water welling up to eternal life."[9]

Likewise he also described himself as "the bread of life"[10] and the deep satisfaction of a hunger which has been fed is reflected in Augustine's prayer, "You have created us for yourself, and our hearts are restless until we find our rest in you."[11]

Perhaps it is because this spiritual hunger is not fed in those who hold the keys to the world's resources that the power of greed rules with a rod of iron. Because I have begun by emphasising spiritual poverty as well as material poverty, please do not assume that I am trying to evoke sympathy for the rich! As I have said, the Kingdom of God is about roots and not just fruit and Jesus wants to lay his axe to the roots of trees which are not producing godly fruit. True, God does care about the lostness of Howard Hughes-type figures – those who seem to have everything, but really have nothing[12] – but these people usually have the power to do something about their situation. The poor usually do not.

2. The Idol of Material Prosperity

> "I used to think, when I was a child, that Christ might have been exaggerating when he warned about the dangers of wealth. Today I know better. I know how very hard it is to be rich and stll keep the milk of human kindness. Money has a dangerous way of putting scales on one's eyes, a dangerous way of freezing people's hands, eyes, lips and hearts. (Dom Helder Camara)[13]

The second root of materialistic madness is the way in which we view economics as a whole. An economist himself, Tim Cooper notes that the words "ecology" and "economics" both share the same Greek root of *oikos* meaning surroundings or house.[14] Ecology is the *study* of these surroundings, whilst economics refers to their *management*. Common sense dictates that the study should precede the management, but sadly Western society has approached the *oikos* back to front! Economics has been developed into an elaborate social science over many years (a wag once described the subject as "common sense made difficult") whilst ecology is a mere academic babe. In other words, the cart of industrial progress and development has been been placed firmly before the horse of understanding the world which we are developing.

Since the eighteenth century the idea of "progress" has been linked with material well-being and comfort. Sadly, the undoubted technological advances of the past two centuries (some of which are definitely welcome and some of which are definitely not) have been made at a very high price to the earth. Every product has manufacturing, packaging, transport and other costs which the producer will carefully consider before it is launched. However, until recently the environmental costs simply did not appear in the equation. Pollution, plundering of non-renewable resources, careless disposal of waste, and the wider impact of the product are all relatively invisible factors to the businessman and his economist.

I would like to argue that the bottom-line reason for this is that members of the general public want what they get, as Paul Weller's song says.[15] The consumer is very happy just to keep on consuming and generally asks few questions about how the product arrived on the shop-shelf, or whether the purchase is really a sensible investment. In fact, the level of consumerism in the West is completely out of control. The futility and totally depraved nature of the present state of affairs is best illustrated by the Californian bumper sticker which reads, "the one with the most toys when he dies wins"!

Many Christians are beginning to explain this in the biblical term of idolatry. There is certainly something very powerful about the impact of material progress and about money itself. Money somehow motivates people and creates this obsession for more; it would almost seem that materialism has gained a life of its own in Western industrial cultures. This is the conclusion of the Dutch writer, Bob Goudzwaard,

> "The goal of material prosperity requires us to adjust our behaviour to its means – continuous economic growth. We have become dependent on economic growth, and it has ensnared us. Though initially a relatively innocent tool, it has become established as a power against us. It coerces us and reveals to us what we must do to survive.'[16]

This is thoroughly typical of the impact of idols and mirrors the experience of God's people in the Old Testament. It is one of the reasons why God forbad them to his people Israel[17] and to the Church. The only way to destroy the grip of an idol is to turn away from it and turn to God himself.[18] In this sense, the issues of spiritual poverty and idol worship are closely linked: only the Lord God can offer true meaning and true liberation in life. One wonders, whilst God's Spirit is restoring prophetic ministry in Britain, whether an Amos or an Hosea will be raised up to declare:

> "I hate, I despise your religious feasts;
> I cannot stand your assemblies.
> Even though you bring me burnt offerings and grain offerings,
> I would not accept them . . .
> Away with the noise of your songs!
> I will not listen to the music of your harps.
> But let justice roll on like a river,
> Righteousness like a never-ending stream!"[19]

It would seem that whilst we should be grateful to God

for lively, exciting and relevant worship, there is a priority on economic righteousness and social justice.

Greed is Good

As we emerge from the yuppie decade of the 1980s, the problems it left in its wake are coming home to roost. Nigel Lawson's "tax giveaway" budget of 1988 heralded a spending spree in Britain which proved to be short-lived, fuelled inflation and eventually required a squeezed national economy. This in turn has created more unemployment, high interest rates and business failures by the minute. It was ironically a US film, *Wall Street*, which put into the mouth of the lead character, Gordon Gekko, the epitaph of those years: "greed is good; greed is right; greed works." Accumulation of as many "toys" as possible is life's chief goal.

Greed did almost become a virtue in the 1980s and this is where the grip of idols can be most easily seen. What is more, there is so much around us which encourages greed. In *Going Underground*, Paul Weller was saying that people not only want more and more, but that *what* they want is dictated by the producers themselves. The manipulative work of the salesman and the advertising industry skillfully create desires that may never have been dreamt of twenty years ago. If you have ever sat through a timeshare promotion (not exactly hell, but an experience close to it, I imagine) or some other "hard sell" exercise, you too will have felt abused and cheapened.

Television advertisements are a more subtle version of the same thing. Products, like money itself, are said to offer power, success and comfort. It has been said that the aim of the advertiser is to rob you of your dignity and sell it back at the price of the product. You might buy your sexuality for the price of a car, some perfume, or a soft-porn magazine; or your self-esteem for the price of a perm, a pint of lager, or a packet of slim panatellas.

Of course, the justification behind "greed is good" is that the more wealth created, the more there is to be shared out. Sadly, the ideal of the market economy where everyone has a chance to make it to the top is fatally flawed. The model of a game is quite appropriate in many ways. Injustices are inbuilt; everyone starts at a different place on the board, and some never have the chance to pass "go", let alone collect £200!

Greed has not created more wealth; rather the credit boom which financed our avarice has created more debt. A 1991 report, *Escaping the Debt Trap*,[20] revealed that over five million people in Britain were in serious or multiple debt, and over 800,000 families in rent or mortgage arrears. The level of consumer credit was over £50 billion at the end of 1990, double the 1982 figure and the average adult now owes over £1,000! These problems have contributed to many other ills in our society – homelessness, family breakdown and an increase of crime.

Taking a biblical view, there has clearly been a tragic confusion between the world's view of wholeness – a full pay-packet, a well-equipped house and a foreign holiday – and the Kingdom vision of *shalom*. Once again, the Church has failed to distinguish itself properly from the consumer treadmill on which we walk but make little progress.

If this all sounds rather too political,[21] then we may need to remind ourselves of the commandment which our culture has conveniently forgotten:

> "You shall not covet your neighbour's house. You shall not covet your neighbour's wife, or his manservant or maidservant, his ox or donkey, or anything that belongs to your neighbour."[22]

If we reject dualism, then we must allow the Bible to challenge even the most ingrained habits and expectations of our society. This in turn must cause us to reject the selfish coveting and lusting after that which we do not have and our neighbour does. If we are to call a spade a spade, few of us can deny that this is one commandment which we are constantly tripping over.

One World is Enough

If the mishandling of money on the home front is bad, with injustice, excess and homelessness mixed together beneath the surface of national life, the global scene is staggering. Most of us probably feel numbed and powerless when we think about world poverty. It is hard to imagine one billion hungry people while we tuck into yet another warm, filling meal.

The contrast of the 1980s was that the decade of greed in Britain was also a decade of mass compassion. The Band Aid charity, conceived by Bob Geldof, raised thousands of millions of pounds for famine relief in Africa. Beginning in 1985, it went on to raise several more billions of pounds over the following years with Live Aid, Run the World and so on. The work has been continued in the entertainments world with Comic Relief. No doubt part of the energy which supported these projects was a desire to do *something* to stem this feeling of powerlessness. If, like me, you have worn a red nose and phoned in your Access number on these kinds of events you will know what I mean.

Yet tragically, the same media which enables these events to raise finance tends to mask the whole story. The News which we see, hear and read is not necessarily *the* news, but it is what we apparently want to receive. Millions may be turning to Christ in China and thousands dying of typhoid in Thailand, but all we are told is what Princess Di is wearing to the races! A famine may be a media event, but apparently one billion hungry people every day is not.

Even when tragedies such as famines are reported, the picture is often distorted. We are led to believe that these famines are inevitable and the result of "natural" disasters. This is only part of the story, and sadly the outrage against suffering and the generosity of a "Red Nose Day" soon wear off.

Before looking at some practical responses which we can all make to the topsy-turvey world of money, let's expand the poverty wide-angled lens. The following thumb-nail sketch offers a simplified picture of how the problems arose and why they are not inevitable.

Development

When the countries of Asia, Africa and Latin America emerged from their domination by European powers after the Second World War, each of them was eager to make material progress. Few of them were ready or able to turn the clocks back to the years before colonialisation. Political influences and models may have differed, but the goals of growth were set in stone. Eager to compete with their former masters, from Guyana to Ghana and New Guinea, economies were quickly geared to ensure that equality could be grasped.

Debt

Naturally, this growth had to be paid for. In the 1970s the northern banks and the International Monetary Fund (IMF) were willing to lend money on a vast scale to developing countries. Banks were rather bad at looking at nations' ability to repay, or at the purpose of the loans. The ruthless (and sometimes brainless) approach of some of the banks was best summarized by Walter Wriston, former president of Citibank, who declared that the debts would never go bad, as "countries do not fail to exist". Perhaps Mr Wriston was getting confused. If a poor hire-purchase debtor fails to make his payments, his Ford Escort may be properly taken back by the finance company. Translating the scenario onto a global scale is slightly more problematic – can you imagine repossessing Peru?

However, interest rates soared and the price of cash crops (like sugar, coffee and copper) fell. This has put tremendous pressure upon the debtor nations, to the point that over one trillion US dollars are now owed to the banks.

Defence

At the same time, many of the new, fragile and inexperienced nations fell into the leadership of dictators who became more interested in power than progress. Vast amounts of borrowed money have been spent on weapons of war, producing misery, not wealth, for these nations.

Even in those countries which did not become absorbed with their military machines, the money has often been "blown" in other ways. Some governments embarked upon enormous projects which were not only costly but were sometimes useless; others like Chile went on a spending spree of consumerism; whilst most were (unwisely) encouraged to industrialise at all costs. The scourge of corruption was constantly in the mix as was the ever present need for back-handers to the boys.

Deterioration

At the level of personal debt, many of us know that if we allow our credit card account to remain unpaid, compound interest means that it gradually becomes a monster, growing further and further out of control. After more than a decade of exorbitant interest rates, dozens of nations like Egypt, the Philippines, Zaire and Mexico face more than mounting debts – they are in a debt trap. The horror of this trap is shown by returning to the subject of Band Aid. In 1985 approximately £2500 million was raised for famine relief in Africa. In the same year the famine stricken countries paid back to Northern banks, governments and agencies double this sum in debt repayments.[23] Now that's what I call news!

In response to this, the IMF have moved in and imposed their own brilliant schemes to help these countries to gear their economies to spend less on themselves and repay more to the bankers. Officially described as "adjustment", they are more accurately and popularly known as "austerity" programmes. The net result of many of these programmes is that imports are slashed, and production is geared to exports. When Britain's imports go down it usually means we are buying fewer Japanese video players and fewer German cars; for these poorer countries it often means less food. It is no exaggeration to say that the debt trap is killing people.

Austerity is not the only string attached to the revised loan structures. Some private overseas debts have been taken over by government-owned financial organisations. These agencies have made arrangements with indebted developing nations that often involve controlling their trading patterns. An example of this might be, "we will write off one year's interest on your debt if you sell your bananas only to us, and if you buy all your new air force bombers from our arms manufacturers." And we boast about our aid contributions!

Destruction

As if all this were not enough, the IMF programmes also encourage rapid development which is frequently an ecological catastrophe. As Susan George puts it, "Indebted countries have not just borrowed money – they have mortgaged the future."[24] The result has been described as "ecocide". The environment, a hidden victim of the debt crisis, seems to suffer in two particular ways.

First, some of the loans have financed schemes of the least ecologically-friendly kind. One example of this is the World Bank's loan to finance the Tucurui hydro-electric project in Amazonia, Brazil. At an anticipated cost of $8 billion, the dam has resulted in dozens of deaths through the infamous defolient "agent orange", a ravaging impact on the water systems of the rainforest and the resettlement of 30,000 American Indians. A number of smaller dams could have provided the same electricity at far lower human and environmental cost. This is only one of many initiatives which are actively financing the rape of the rainforests.

The second connection with the environment is the need to repay these loans. As Brazil has to find between $12 and $14 billion every year in interest payments there is obviously a pressing need for cash crops, like soyabeans, to be grown for export. To grow these, the big landowners and the government have thrown peasants off the best land to extend their soyabean plantations. The peasants have been moved to areas like Rondonia, where they have been encouraged to slash and burn their way into the forests, displacing indigenous Indians on their way and leaching the land of its goodness.

The 3D Solution

This nightmare scenario of world economics gone crazy is almost too bizarre to believe. The rich Northern economies are being financed by the debt-servicing of the starving South. The situation is coming to resemble the scene from Joseph Heller's satire, *Catch 22*, in which Milo explains one of his more intricate business deals and finally says, "Look, its very simple: I'm the people I buy from"!

However infuriating and alarming the situation is, we must not despair – answers can and must be found. The so-called 3D solution involves reviewing the whole structure of *debts*. The strings attached by the bankers must be broken; a moratorium must be agreed on interest payments; austerity packages must be scrapped. There also needs to be a true encouragement of *democracy*. To be frank, for all their rhetoric about democracy, Western powers have been rather too willing to uphold brutal and discredited regimes in the past – Pinochet in Chile, the Shah in Iran and Marcos in the Philippines – whilst the debts are being serviced. Finally, the emphasis must be placed on *development*. Proper development of Third World economies will involve carefully-planned growth which does not cripple a nation, exploit its people and ruin its ecology.

On top of all this, major changes must be made to the way in which world trade operates. Patterns which have changed little since the days of empires still seem to dominate the weaker and poorer nations. If anything, the trading blocs which are being developed in different parts of the globe are tending to further harm the position of Third World countries. The 1990s may be a decade of opportunity in Europe, but could be a decade of disaster for others as non-Europeans are shut out in trading terms.

Where the Buck Stops

I began the chapter by emphasising the need to make connections. With an issue so huge and seemingly remote as the Third World debt crisis, how can it affect us and can we do anything about it? The answer to this question lies in the source of our power as Christians.

I believe in the power of the Holy Spirit – God does want to empower us in many different ways. The sense of power*less*ness which we all feel from time to time in our own lives – emotionally, spiritually and even physically – is something that God himself can transform. Recovering a more wholistic gospel will mean that we can call upon the Holy Spirit not just to perform signs and wonders, healings and salvation. We will also call upon him to help us in *all* areas of "our weakness".[25]

Rather than just shoving the questions of financial injustice and material excess under the carpet, I believe that the Spirit wants us to consider action. On a broad level, by adopting the standards of living which our society accepts as normal, we fuel the drive for more and more economic growth. This means that as a nation we consume more and more of the earth's resources, put more and more pressure on the poorer nations and squeeze the fragile ecological balance of our planet tighter. Thus, lifestyle is a key.

As Ronald Sider noted in his 1977 classic, *Rich Christians in an Age of Hunger*, "We affluent Westerners have a problem". The problem is that we think we can hardly get by on the ten, fifteen or twenty thousand pounds that we earn. This is the rat race. We must turn from the sin of covetousness, and the idolatry of materialism. God certainly has a view on this; his anger burns against injustice,

> "Seek the Lord and live . . . You trample on the poor and force him to give you grain."[26]

It must begin with you and with me. We have the power to make the difference if we will only choose to do so.

Put plainly, if we do not live more simply, the poor simply will not live.

Turn, Turn, Turn

How can we do this – translate an emotional plea into solid action? First, we need to repent. The New Testament word "repent" is translated from the Greek *metanoia*, meaning to change one's mind after thought.[27] Apart from the Bible, the word was used as a military command for changing direction when marching, equivalent to, "about TURN!" Its most common use in the Church is the idea of an unbeliever turning from sin to faith and trust in Christ.

However, as I suggested in Chapter 6, changing of the mind is a continuous process for the Christian. Therefore repentance needs to be an on-going part of our lives. In our generation, repentance from materialism, idolatry and covetousness are essential. We must decide we are going to think and act differently. The whole Church needs to repent collectively, but we must begin individually.

Better to Give

Second, and as a practical out-working of repentance, we must recover the art of giving. Giving is in the heart of God himself, who not only gave us this wonderful earth as a present, and generously answers our prayers, but "gave his one and only Son"[29] for the world he so loves. Having established in Chapter 3 that stewardship is about more than money, I must say that it will affect our money! " 'The silver is mine and the gold is mine,' declares the Lord Almighty" through the prophet Haggai.[30] Our relative affluence puts upon us a burden of responsibility to use this money with great wisdom – and great generosity.

A society which covets goods encourages us to hold on tightly to our cash. All the teaching of the Bible points us in the opposite direction. From the limited accumulation of wealth allowed by the Jubilee principle, through Jesus' comments on riches and the Kingdom of God[32] to the dynamic radicalism of the early church,[33] the emphasis of stewardship and gratitude to God should cause us to keep a light hold on possessions. The act of giving – of financial sacrifice – will not mean that God owes us a favour, but that we live a freer life.

How then should we give? The Bible teaches clearly that when believers give it should be a recognition that all we have "belongs to the Lord"[34] Our giving is an "overflowing [of] many expressions of thanks to God".[35] Because the Lord does not have his own bank account number, this finance is to be given to people. The first place a Christian will look to is their local church: in the Old Testament we see the spiritual leaders, the Levites, being supported by the people's tithes (that is one tenth of all income).[36] In the New Testament the parallel is gifts laid "at the apostles' feet."[37] We have also seen that goods and money were swiftly passed around where a need was recognised. Practically, this kind of giving will enable the Church to function more effectively as an agent of God's Kingdom, and will be a tremendously positive witness to the local community.

However, we should also take opportunities to express our faith on a more global basis. Through aid agencies like Tear Fund, Cafod, Christian Aid and Oxfam there is a direct opening for us to support on-going development and relief projects in the world's poorer nations. They also give us an invaluable window on this "other world" that we have heard about and seen via the television, but which can still seem safely distant from us. Before we were married, Charlotte "sponsored" a child through a Tear Fund scheme. Her name is Maria and she is the daughter of a subsistence farmer on the Caribbean island of Haiti. We receive simple letters about twice a year: one Christmas she politely thanked us for money given as a present writing, "I bought a goat". It seemed a reasonable investment to us!

By diverting our money into the Church and into constructive projects in the Third World, we can make our own small prophetic statements about reversing the flow of finance from debt-servicing. But this alone will not be enough. Let our giving not become a sop to our consciences, allowing us to carry on in the same way for, "from everyone who has been given much, much will be demanded."[38]

I believe that part of the "much" which God will demand of Western Christians will be a resistance of the ever-rising ceiling of "needs" with which the advertising machine bombards us. If last year's need was a video-player and this year's is a CD – what will it be next? The treadmill never stops; but we can get off. I am not suggesting that we adopt a boring, spartan existence, but why not build in our own ceilings? What about setting a faith goal that we can *resist* getting a larger and more powerful car, rather than asking God to "bless us" with one?

These things do need to be planned in advance and kept under constant review. When we were still students and owned little more than the duffle coats and leg-warmers we stood in, Lotty and I chatted one day about the way we would live if we ever got married. With all the noble naivete of youth, we decided there and then that our goal would not be the trappings of middle-class success, but the values of the Kingdom of God. Ten years later, as I look around our home, we have seen some success and some failure. Our God is a God who loves to give, and to shun his generosity is not mature but arrogant and super-spiritual. However, a want can so easily become a need and possessions can so easily possess. Let's not carry any excess baggage – it's sure to cost us more and slow us down!

How Green is "Green"?

Before leaving the subject of consumerism I must warn of a subtle snare to the environment-conscious. Panicked by the sudden awareness of the public to such subjects as phosphates, recycling and CFC gases, manufacturers have been quick to change the packaging and labelling of their products. The statistics are quite remarkable. In 1988 a MORI opinion poll asked whether people had bought a product because they thought it was "green" and 18% of those asked said that they had. By May 1989 this figure had gone up to 42%.[39] In spite of this fact – or perhaps because of it – for many companies the greening of their image has been a higher priority than improving their product range.

Whilst it is encouraging that individuals are making the connection between what they buy and such problems as global warming, ozone depletion and deforestation, there are two main problems. The first is one of confusion caused by green-labelling. When you are faced with a choice of washing-up liquids or other products, what is different about the ones which claim to be "environmentally-friendly", "ozone-friendly" or even "dolphin-friendly"? There are stories of long-standing brands of cleaner suddenly labelled, "phosphate-free". The joke is that they never ever contained phosphates in the first place! Thanks to the work of pressure groups, the government is amending the Trades Description Act and will soon introduce an official "Eco-label" system.[40]

The second and most important problem is that green consumerism is *still* consumerism. Whether grey or green, consumerism fuels demand, uses resources and pollutes. A greater enemy than all the phosphates, non-biodegradable plastic and virgin pulp put together, the rate at which we devour the products is the heart of the matter. It is right to consume better, but we must also consume less.

Summary

Money is an intensely important subject both from a green and from a Christian perspective. Not only is "the love of money a root of all kinds of evil"[41] but most of us reading this book will have a relatively large amount (in global terms) of it flowing through our accounts. It is ironic that in an age where technology has given us the greatest ever power to solve the problems of hunger and disease, there are probably more people dying for want of basic nutrition and clean water today than ever before.

In this chapter I have attempted to show the connection between the pain of the poorer world and the age of greed in which we live. There is nothing glamorous about poverty, and we must beware of a sort of sentimental attitude towards the Third World – there is plenty of sin, greed and exploitation there as well. But when we understand that there is a link between the two it must cause us to get angry with what we see – why can't everyone get their fair share of the cake? As far as we are concerned, the idol of material prosperity is worshipped and the sin of covetousness crouches at the door. This is why I describe greed as the single most significant root of the ecological crisis and call on the Church to show itself distinct from it.

Jesus himself offers us the model of a simple lifestyle – living life to the full yet travelling light without the burden of material wealth. Can we green our lives, not just by filling our cupboards with greener products, but by being radical with our money? If so, we may spare ourselves from the hypocrisy which casts a long shadow over the world economy,

> "I WAS HUNGRY
> and you blamed it on the communists
> I WAS HUNGRY
> and you circled the moon
> I WAS HUNGRY
> and you said God helps those who help themselves
> I WAS HUNGRY
> and you told me that machines do that work now
> I WAS HUNGRY
> and you had napalm bills to pay
> I WAS HUNGRY
> and you said the poor are always with you."[42]

Practical Steps

Personal Finances

- Pray that God will show you how to respond to the global crisis. Stay free from idolising prosperity and coveting in your own lifestyle. Take some time to think about what work and money mean to you. Do you enjoy the things you are paid to do? Which of the things you do give you real satisfaction? What do you give most value to?

- Take a look around your home. Are there any items that you really don't need or use? Could you sell them and give the money to a relief agency, or simply give an object to someone who has more use for it? For me, this means digging out an old stamp collection which is gathering dust, but has some financial value.
- Review your outgoings. How do you spend your weekly or monthly income? Without removing every hint of fun from your life, are there items which you could cut down on, or cut out?
- Give it away! If you are a Christian, seriously consider a regular gift to your local church. We have seen that the tithe, or tenth of income, was usual in the Old Testament, but we can give much more now!

Once we have done this, we should look around us and see if we can help any of our friends or anyone else we know is in need.

Then we should work out how we can support those in need in other parts of the world. I have already referred to child sponsorship, which will cost around £15 per month, but there are plenty of ways to support aid agencies and other charities. You may want to make a regular donation or save some money so that you can respond to emergency appeals.

- Review your investments. If you have a pension, life insurance or shares then your money will be employed in many companies which may be involved in a huge variety of business activities. Given what I have said about stewardship, it is well worth knowing what you are investing in. In the worst cases you could be helping to finance ecocide, virtual slave-labour conditions for workers and dubious products including arms and gambling. Your money may also be working for you in nations ruled by corrupt and evil regimes, using fear and torture to suppress opposition, and mortgaging the future of their environment.

In the best cases, you could be investing in companies which have a strong ethical base and are involved with constructive development projects. There is no substitute for doing your own research, but don't just talk to the companies concerned. There are a number of good ethical investment "packages", where the fund-managers undertake not to invest your money in the arms, tobacco, gambling, or similar industries or in unjust regimes. You can also find a few brokers who specialise in ethical and ecologically-sound investments.

- Think twice about purchasing anything on credit, and only do so if you know (rather than hope) how you can pay off the debt quickly. Use credit cards cautiously. Always make sure you know exactly the terms of the credit arrangement.

Shopping

- Beware of green labelling and green consumerism. Make a list before you go out and stick to it (particularly relevant to the author – "impulse buys" were designed with me in mind!). Get to know what you are looking out for in terms of labelling, ie recycled, non-bleached, local produce, minimum wrapping, and so on, wherever possible.
- Transnational corporations hold Third World producers of raw materials in their grip and are key players in the North/South injustice. By avoiding the huge companies which maintain unfair trade – Unilever, General Foods, Nestle, etc. – your purchasing can bring some fairer trade. There are now over 40 alternative trading organisations working in Britain with well over a quarter of a million customers.[43] Write off to Traidcraft, Tearcraft or Oxfam for a catalogue.
- Remember to ask the question, "do I really need it?" before you ask, "is it green?" Reduced consumerism is better than green consumerism.
- Look at the product's country of origin. If it has been transported half way round the world then a huge amount of energy will have been used en route.

- Use recycyled products
- Buy products in packaging that can be recycled locally
- Avoid over-packaging and have a moan at the store manager when you come across it.
- Buy milk in bottles and return them

Resisting the Advertisers

- Although some are funny, why not switch channels or turn the volume down when the adverts come on. Everyone says, "but adverts don't affect me, I know it's propaganda." If they don't work I'd like to know why companies are prepared to spend six and seven figure sums on each twenty second slot! It's because we're all vegetating in front of the moron magnet that the information slips in. So be on the initiative – press a button.
- You can write to banks, credit card companies and others asking them to stop sending you advertisements. Likewise, write to the Mailing Preference Service informing them you do not wish to receive unsolicited mail. This will save you subjecting yourself to a sales technique and will save some trees and some energy to boot!

Political Action

- As always, you can write to your MP and press him or her for their party's stance on international justice and debt. Register your own concerns over debt and development with your MP and write to the Minister for Overseas Development, again pressing her to take a more just and active line in the debt crisis.
- Keep up to date with what is happening in the world through television and newspapers. You might like to develop a particular interest in one part of the world: learn about what's happening, pray for that nation or area, discover what Christian groups are doing there, and if possible target your finances there. Charlotte and I have done this with Angola in south-west Africa. We hope to visit that nation one day.

- Contact your bank. Most of the big four High Street banks were involved with Third World debts in the 1970s, but deny they are receiving interest payments from developing nations. Write and ask what they have done with these debts. Threaten (as I have done) to move your account to a building society if you are unsatisfied.
- Write to your local newspaper raising the issues of international debt. If you can focus a letter or a press release around some kind of fund-raising event, you may make a great contribution to raising awareness in your area.
- Vote for the party which seems most committed to justice and a fair deal for the Third World.

Church-based action

- Ask your leaders if you can invite someone to speak on the often taboo subject of money in your church or youth group. We have taught on finances in Revelation in a number of ways: looking positively at giving in a series called "We Live to Give" and warning of the dangers of materialism.
- Contact Tear Fund, Cafod or Christian Aid to find out what they do, and how they are seeking to put Christian convictions into action.
- Organise a local fund-raising event which is fun and raises the profile of the issues and the aid agency, and also shows that your church cares.
- Consider involvement as a church with an overseas situation. As I mentioned in Chapter 7, we are fortunate to be developing links with church leaders in Zaire, Romania and Yugoslavia. In time, we hope that these relationships will provide an opportunity to release people and more finance into those needy situations. However, there will be no paternalism – we will greatly benefit from the cultural and spiritual distinctives they can share with us.
- Pray for the world's poor. Taking on this task can seem hopelessly daunting – where do we start? As usual, no easy answers exist apart from asking the Holy Spirit to help us take on God's pain and to begin to plead for our poorer

global neighbours. Ichthus Christian Fellowship are one church which has held prayer retreats to focus on intercession for these situations – praying together seems to be the best way to get started with big issues.[44]

Notes

1 Perhaps the all-time pop classic is the 1973 Pink Floyd song of the same title (*Money*).
2 Mark 4:9.
3 The phrase "Third World" is deemed to add the insult of inferior status to the injury of economic exploitation. It was coined after the Second World War when the First World was said to be the Western democracies of North America and Europe, the Second World the communist power blocs of Eastern Europe and Asia, with the Third World comprising the rest.
4 The slightly euphemistic phrase "less well developed" is preferred by the UN.
5 The majority of the world's poorest nations are located in the Southern Hemisphere, the majority of the richest are in the Northern Hemisphere. However, it is common for "South" to be used synonymously with "Third World". For example, Christian Aid report that although 75% of the world's population live in the South their share of its income is 20%, of its grain is 33% and of its annually consumed protein is 20%.
6 Penguin, 1988, p xiii.
7 Quoted in Kathy Keay *How To Make The World Less Hungry* IVP 1990 p 24.
8 Quoted in Cooper *Green Christianity* Spire 1990 p 71.
9 John 4:13,14.
10 John 6:35.
11 Quoted in Keay, *ibid.* p 28.
12 To underline the fact of this real poverty, the phrase "up and outs" has been coined, to contrast with the more obvious needs of the "down and outs".
13 Quoted in Sider *Rich Christians in an Age of Hunger* IVP 1977 p 33.
14 Cooper *ibid.* pp 72,73.
15 The Jam *Going Underground* Virgin Records, 1980.
16 Bob Goudzwaard *Idols of Our Time* IVP 1984.
17 See Exodus 20:4–6.
18 1 John 5:21.
19 Amos 5:21–24.
20 The report was published by the economics group of the Movement for Christian Democracy and reported in *The Times*, 22 October 1991.

21 The fact that the Conservatives governed Britain during the 1980s is perhaps less significant than is sometimes thought: all the other major political parties favour increased economic growth.
22 Exodus 20:17.
23 From J Bennett *The Hunger Machine* Polity, 1987.
24 *A Fate Worse Than Debt*, *Ibid*. p 155.
25 Romans 8:26.
26 Amos 5:6,11.
27 W E Vine *Expository Dictionary of New Testament Words* p 961.
29 John 3:16.
30 Haggai 2:8.
32 Matthew 19:23; Mark 4:19.
33 Acts 2:45; 4:32.
34 Leviticus 27:30.
35 2 Corinthians 9:12.
36 Eg Numbers 18:31.
37 Acts 4:35,37.
38 Luke 12:48.
39 Friends of the Earth.
40 Friends of the Earth briefing sheet *Green Consumerism* June 1990.
41 1 Timothy 6:10.
42 From an Asian Christian Conference on Development, quoted in Keay, ibid., p.47.
43 John Button *How To Be Green* Century 1989, p.205.
44 For more information of the Ichthus initiative contact Roger Mitchell at Ichthus Christian Fellowship, 107 Stanstead Road, Forest Hill, London SE23 1HH.

Chapter 10

SEEING GREEN FOR JESUS' SAKE

Working out our environmental ethic

Questions and Answers

In 1659 the French thinker Blaise Pascal said, "Working hard to think clearly is the beginning of moral conduct." Whilst I have tried to give the activists plenty to get their teeth into (and we all need to be active about the things we believe in), this book is primarily addressed to the way in which we think. God has given us moral instincts and intuition to guide us, but it will be our *thinking* that determines where we are actually going. The mind is not just the preserve of academics and intellectuals – it's part of each person's makeup, equipping us to make reasoned decisions. Whether or not we admit it, thought precedes action. That is why questions are a helpful provocation.

Asking questions can be quite threatening: we don't always like the answers we receive; we might appear to be uncertain about what we are doing and we might get drawn into debates that we would rather not face. Indeed, many people do not face the tough questions of life because they fear that the final answers may be rather inconvenient! For example, it is because conversion involves a choice, and that making such a choice can be most uncomfortable, that some individuals will probably always prefer to reject Christ's offer of salvation.

I remember how disturbed I felt when a friend asked me what I was going to actually *do* about my professed faith in Jesus (this friend was clearly not impressed by my lifestyle at the time!). Without this direct challenge, I might have happily fudged and compromised my way through life. God himself has the habit of asking naggingly pertinent questions like "Where are you?" to Adam,[1] "But who do you say I am?" to the disciples,[2] and "Why are you testing me, you hypocrites?"[3] to the Pharisees!

Whilst evangelistic preachers are quick to ask their unbelieving listeners to make sober assessments about their lives, Christians and church leaders are certainly not always an exception to the rule of "ignorance is bliss". Whether a very traditional church with a conservative agenda ("if the Book of Common Prayer was good enough for Wesley, it's good enough for me"), or a radical, church-planting, youth-oriented expression of church (pump-up-the-volume worship, loud T-shirts and pony-tails), rocking the boat is guaranteed to make you unpopular. The reasons for this are many: fear of the unknown, inflexible structures and fear of losing sight of the goal being among them.

Sadly, those churches that seem to be best at asking the right questions often fail to tie healthy self-assessment with clear God-given vision and a humble attitude. This can result in cynicism, intellectualism and following the worst example of the people of Israel, ". . . everyone did what was right in his own eyes."[4]

On the other hand, it is far easier to make statements than to ask questions. When I make a bold assertion of truth, I sound far more certain and convincing and I feel more secure. Unfortunately, statements can be aggressive and defensive – questions invite reflection; statements close debate down. Approaching the controversial subject of green-ness I have not wanted to issue a command to "go green" - that would have prejudged the matter. Perhaps it would also have ignored the biblical prohibition against "passing judgement on disputable matters."[5]

Aware of this tension, I have tried to make this book a question to the Church and a challenge to those in the Green movement who have not accepted Jesus as Christ. To ask "how green is your gospel?" does not hide a pre-determined answer. It is not a statement disguised as a question, but a question which can never have a definitive answer for all times and places.

Tough Questions

Because this is a book about ideas intended to provoke response and promote action, I do not wish to end it with a morass of facts and information about what you must do next. In the appendices following this chapter there are details of many excellent resources available to help us to take more steps to live greener lives.

Instead, let's consider some final questions.

1. How can I include environmental concerns within my faith?

There is a danger of tacking "green issues" onto the agenda of the Church, like a sort of trendy badge. The buzz issues of the past decades – worship, evangelism, relationships, spiritual warfare, the role of women and so on – have been faced and "taken on board" to differing degrees in different cases. Because of our culture's tendency to compartmentalise life, it is only too easy to pigeonhole a subject and dispose of it painlessly on the one hand, or do a pendulum swing and throw everything into it on the other! The essence of grasping a greener gospel will be that we are willing to embrace a more wholistic view of life. This in turn will leave nothing else untouched. It will be something like the table on which the jigsaw of life is pieced together.

"Embracing a more wholistic view of life" sounds sort of vague and complex – and it is! That is why I feel a bit uncomfortable with the "be green or be damned" approach which lays out a checklist of criteria to help you qualify for green credibility. Rather, we must engage in a subjective process which involves the Spirit of God, faith, prayer and our friends. It will mean that all our actions and our priorities are assessed according to a wide variety of factors. These include obedience to the Holy Spirit at all times; biblical morality – honesty, faithfulness, forgiveness and so on; our duty to love our neighbour and our responsibility as stewards made in the image of God.

Most of the time, taking on a positive environmental stance will not cut across any other aspect of our Christian faith and church life. At times we will have to ask questions of ourselves and one another – questions like, "what motivates me" and "why do we do things this way?" At times we will be faced with clashing priorities, which are discussed below. Whatever, nobody ever promised that Christianity, or life itself, was going to be totally simple. All I know is that God promises to give us wisdom when we ask[7] – and we don't need "A" levels to do that!

2. Isn't environmentalism becoming like a righteousness in itself?

The New Testament teaching on law and grace shows that we cannot work towards the Lord through our own righteousness. Only Jesus has paved the way for us to be restored to friendship with God by taking the punishment for our sins, and by giving us a new righteousness – a fresh start. This is why Paul writes,

> ". . . if anyone is in Christ, he is a new creation; the old has gone, the new has come!"[8]

This righteousness can only be *received*, never earned. It is a *gift* of grace, or undeserved favour, from God to the beloved fallen monarchs of his creation. All good work that a Christian does should flow out of a gratitude to God for his love and generosity in saving us and giving us this new beginning. Yet somehow there seems to be a great desire in humanity to try to earn and deserve this righteousness through personal effort. Rules and regulations are so easily added to make us feel that there is a "higher standard" of Christianity which we are just not quite reaching. This kind of "Jesus plus" faith is often described as legalism – that is, to be a proper Christian you need to receive

Jesus *plus* pray every day, *plus* smile all the time, *plus* never use rude words or whatever.

The temptation towards legalism is not new. When first century Galatian Christians were falsely taught that they needed to receive Jesus *plus* be circumcised, the Apostle Paul got quite cross,

> "You foolish Galatians, who has bewitched you? . . . As for those agitators, I wish they would go the whole way and emasculate themselves!"[9]

Regardless of how one views New Age infiltration of the Green movement, when people grow convinced of the need for environmental commitment they usually become quite passionate. A high level of motivation seems to be generated and the vision of a better world is strongly pursued. The challenge for green Christians is to avoid a "Jesus plus environmentalism" righteousness. If some Christians do not share my convictions on ecology, they should not be made to feel in any way inferior. Further, if unbelievers come to our meetings and feel that they have to become green before they can become Christians, we are worse off than the Galatians!

3. How do we prioritise?

I mentioned earlier that occasional clashes of priorities concerning green action are inevitable. However, these are often over-exaggerated and sometimes reveal inconsistent attitudes. "I haven't got time to go to the bottle-bank" is as bad as saying, "I'm too busy to pray"! The resource that every one of us has is time. *We* choose how we spend it – usefully or wastefully; selfishly or generously. If we are at work or school, someone else will probably determine how we spend a lot of our day, but most of us usually still have quite a bit left as well. I know we all say it, but "I haven't got time" just is not true.

In our heart of hearts, most of us know that this phrase generally disguises, "I can't be bothered," or "it's not important enough." No matter how spiritual or sincere our language may be, this is really what is being said. Let us unmask one or two more well-worn phrases.

"It's good stewardship to buy the cheapest product, not the greenest."

The key word here is "stewardship". In religious jargon, stewardship does not mean a wholistic caring for the earth but becomes a camouflage for stinginess. "Cheapest" is another interesting word. The reason that you are shelling out less for the product might be because a Third World manufacturer or the earth itself is paying a higher price. I would suggest that even if church money is involved, true stewardship will always look for more than a short-term return.

"I have to live the same material lifestyle as my friends so I can adequately share the gospel with them."

There is no merit in being cranky, mean or taking little care of our appearance and our property. These are characteristics which *will* discredit our witness to Jesus. However, this does not mean that we have to ape our neighbours' materialism to relate to them. The sermon on the mount is about the values which the followers of Jesus must share – values a pole apart from those of the world system. Jesus himself appeared to have no problem in relating across huge social and cultural divides, yet he chose to live the simplest of lifestyles. What enabled him to communicate his good news was the wholeness and quality of his inner life.

"I don't get involved in environmental groups because they might clash with church meetings and distract me from witnessing to my friends."

This statement hides a number of problems. Firstly, if my interpretation of the "salt of the earth"[10] is correct, involvement in society should not be seen as a danger, but as part of the essential role of the Church.

In the past, there have been Christians who have felt strongly about green issues and joined a local environmental group. Sometimes their church leaders have been confused and a little unsure about the group and have therefore been unable to offer the support needed by these individuals. This has led them to feel "out on a limb" and at times a sense of disapproval. They have seen that their choice lies between drifting from the church to get stuck into the group, or withdrawing from the group to get stuck into the church. Both these alternatives are inadequate to say the least.

As a church leader, I passionately believe in a healthy and active local church: caring for one another, reaching out in evangelism and church-planting, maturing in its understanding of God himself. However, the work of the Church should not be separated from involvement in society. If all our energies are taken up with maintaining the local church or "doing church things" then we are hardly going to be a dynamic force for social change.

Secondly, the idea of "witnessing", as commonly used in Christian circles, is rather a strange one. Witnessing is not something that one can truly go out and physically *do*. We are all witnessing whether we like it or not – the issue really is whether we are good or bad witness!

Naturally, talking about the Lord is a good witness, but most of Jesus' own evangelism involved doing things, and then answering people's questions. Actions always speak louder than words, and life provides us with a wealth of rich opportunities to act. When as a local church we spent one Sunday morning collecting litter in our town, we got into some very interesting conversations. As we demonstrated to local residents the care which Jesus had for people, for their environment and for the whole earth, was this not witnessing?

We must not cop out of evangelism – telling people plainly about their need to receive Christ personally – but we must also seek to broaden our witness to the living Christ. This ties in our words and actions into something powerful and meaningful.

There are no doubt many other phrases that you can think of which are used to mask fudged priorities. You might even be thinking of some of your own favourites!

I have already stated that prioritising is rarely straightforward. In Chapter 5, I pointed out that in the case of the Gadarene demoniac, Jesus *does* seem to put the sanity of one tormented man above the lives of a herd of pigs. In contrast, many people are concerned that the British public appear to be more willing to give their money to help a stray dog than to a homeless person. These two illustrations show priorities in action. We may not like the way that other people make their decisions but each of us must face the same questions and decide what is important *for us.*

This has been a problem as some have looked at the green movement. Because the issues are so large, people can be led to believe that it's "in for a penny, in for a pound." In other words, if you can't go the whole way then you're not green at all. This should not be the way it is. The real question is, whose priorities are we following? Those of our prejudices and our own interests, or those of the Kingdom?

4. Does it make sense?

Just as the decisions about how to take green action are sometimes complex, so too are some of the actions themselves. On a global level, environmental awareness has been criticised as a Western middle-class obsession. There is something slightly embarrassing about the thought of wealthy Europeans lecturing Brazilians about the dangers of global warming. For someone relocated from a squalid shanty-town into the Amazonian development zone, their concern is personal survival. In contrast, our concern seems like nothing more than an idea.

At an individual level the same paradoxes apply. Have you ever thought about all the energy used to drive your car full of paper, cans and bottles to the recycling point? Have you ever wondered whether that bit extra you pay for recycled paper would be better spent planting a new tree? What about all the extra time you have to spend in the supermarket reading the labels of the products that you buy. Could that not be spent more usefully?

Whether locally or globally, real tensions and paradoxes do exist. The answer has to be the same in all situations. The people of the Kingdom must seek to live out a prophetic lifestyle as God's stewards on the earth. A prophetic lifestyle means living in a way that carries the message of *shalom* which Jesus' gospel contains. It means wrestling to bring a wholistic approach to every question.

For the Brazilians, short-sighted development will hurt them and their children more than anyone. Applying political pressure for justice on their behalf and giving non-patronising education to empower the people must be the way forward. At home, we must use recycling facilities and campaign for them to be more and more localised. We don't always have to make a special journey with our bottles, etc. We might have to make a slight detour, it might be slightly inconvenient, but doing worthwhile things often are.

5. It sounds good, but can we make a difference?

Right back in Chapter 1 I stated that the magnitude of the ecological crisis is a turn-off to many people. When we talk about climatic changes, one trillion dollars worth of Third World debts and thousands of square miles of rain forest being eaten up each year, feelings of despondency can easily creep in. After all, isn't talk of "lighting a candle in the darkness" just rhetoric? Can the economics of greed and the power of injustice ever be eliminated or overwhelmed in "this dark world"?[11]

There is no premium on ignorance or naivete. Anyone who thinks that tackling these issues will be easy could probably be persuaded that "gullible" is not in the dictionary! Our eyes must be wide open to the powers that we are taking on when we confront the roots of the crisis. These powers are rich, spiritual and very powerful!

The Way Forward

I have already said that we must be quite clear about what we are trying to do. *We* cannot save the planet alone, *we* cannot eliminate the sins of selfishness or covetousness, *we* cannot topple the idols of materialism, security and nationalism. What we *can* do is seek the Kingdom of God – his rule in our lives, in our churches, and in our communities. This will surely make a difference. It made a difference to the slave trade when William Wilberforce took on that power; it made a difference to child labour when Lord Shaftesbury took on the exploitation and abuses of industry; it made a difference to East London when William Booth took on the powers which degraded working people and robbed them of their dignity.

But the goal is only part of our motivation to act. As the songwriter has said, "the way we do things counts for more than we achieve."[12] If we are only going to look for short-term results, I believe we will be bitterly disappointed. A prophetic people will want to demonstrate the ways of God because they are right *per se*. If this earth does belong to the Lord, then he will certainly seek an accounting for the way in which it has been used. I cannot give an account for the way in which Nestle, the Church of England or the National Trust have used their resources – I can only account for what has passed through my hands.

Further, we are also trying to recover a gospel which is whole and understandable. As so many people are grasping the reality of a whole earth of which humanity is no more than a very significant part, an anthropocentric Christian faith shoots itself in the foot every time. Recovering and preaching a gospel of Jesus Christ – Creator and Redeemer – will enable our message to be more easily received by a whole generation. Surely this is music to the evangelist's ears!

Starting our real preaching at the fall is no longer good enough. We should be asking ourselves questions like, "what would I be doing if humanity had not fallen?" I am sure that we would still be students, bankers, teachers, dustmen, sports personalities, entertainers and so on. We would all be living fully for the glory of God though. What one cannot escape when reading the Bible is that it begins in a garden and ends in a city. Progress and development are not wrong, just the sin that distorts its means and its motives. We have got a positive message to preach – a message of hope and of truth.

Some Models

Every idea needs to be earthed. With green ideas both that statement and its metaphor are particularly appropriate! Before concluding, let's briefly observe how green ideas can be implemented at different levels, and how the Church can play its role in the greening of the globe. Below are listed a few models of organisations and communities which are actively trying to tie green perspectives to what and who they actually are. We all need models to get us started. Only a few of these models reflect the work of Christians and none is yet perfect, but all provide both an example and inspiration.

A Nation: New Zealand

With wide political and economic powers, national governments are clearly in a very strong position to influence, direct and implement environmental action. For the many reasons which have been outlined earlier, the instincts of most societies are now towards economic growth at any cost. However, there are signs that one or two nations are prepared to take on the tough questions and face some ecological priorities. One such nation is New Zealand.

Richard Kennaway, a senior university lecturer in Christchurch, New Zealand, has observed that it is not only the huge economic heavyweights that can make a difference to the international response to the present crisis.[13] Citing the example of Malta, which helped to get the Law of the Sea negotiations under way, he notes that nations of any size can take on a role of facilitator/participant, leader/initiator and/or example. New Zealand has played a significant role as a participant and an example in a range of environmental issues. These include playing a crucial part in negotiating the final formula of the 1987 Montreal Protocol on ozone depletion, the suspension of US nuclear ship visits to New Zealand ports in the early 1970s and raising the question of Japanese drift-netting in the South Pacific in 1989. Kennaway rightly notes that to avoid hypocrisy in their international diplomacy New Zealand must continue to give attention to its rising energy consumption at home.

In contrast to this, it is lamentable that successive British governments appear to have done the acceptable minimum both at home and concerning international issues. The most recent White Paper on the Environment is a classic example. All the right words and phrases are there, but very little can be found of substantial commitment. In a democracy, I believe we should be doing all we can to put pressure on the government to address the wide range of concerns where action is urgently required: investment in public transport, pollution taxes, energy efficiency subsidies and so on.

A Project: Reforestation in Nicaragua

It is encouraging to note that in some parts of the world Christians are on the frontline of environmental action.

Because of the close relationship between ecological problems and the suffering of the poor, the Council of Evangelical Churches in Nicaragua (CEPAD) have actively engaged in working with local people to reverse the trend of deforestation. Nicaragua has lost almost two-thirds of its tropical forest in the past forty years and many communities have directly experienced the resulting droughts, floods and soil erosion. Yet when peasants were first encouraged to clear the forests for farm-land and cattle-ranching in the 1950s and 1960s, trees were seen as the enemy. For this reason CEPAD have embarked on education and advice programmes and setting up community tree nurseries with the assistance of rural volunteers.

This project is not expensive nor greatly complex. What it involves is Christians committed to a vision of the gospel working for the poor and bringing *shalom* wholeness to humanity and to the earth.[14]

A City: Leicester

My childhood memories of walking by a canal foaming with waste industrial detergent, now has an interesting twist. That city was Leicester, and the same Leicester has been appointed by the RSNC, The Wildlife Trusts Partnership,[15] as Britain's first "Environment City".[16] This is in addition to Sheffield, Dundee and Cardiff which have become "Recycling City" for England, Scotland and Wales respectively, and Devon which is "Recycling County"!

These initiatives are to be welcomed as they offer the opportunity to empower individuals and groups within the community to improve their natural, built and social environment. Leicester is addressing these latter themes in detail, along with energy; economy and work; food and agriculture; transport; waste and pollution. Cities have traditionally been seen as the focus of the grey, rather than green, nation which we have developed. Therefore it is appropriate that cities should begin to reverse the trend.

Leicester Environment City has set up eight specialist working groups (SWGs) to plan and launch various initiatives. For example, the Built Environment SWG are proposing a conservation area for part of the surviving old centre of the city, a disability guide to Leicester and "play streets" to improve the opportunities for safe play in the urban environment. Meanwhile, the Transport SWG are investigating a community bicycle project and a Green Ringway: a 23 mile pedestrian and cyclist route around the city.

This is a model which can be adopted regardless of the size of the community. It does not need vast amounts of expertise or bureaucracy, rather a willingness to be imaginative and a commitment to see action taken. It is also a level where local churches can take a very positive lead. Why not find out what local groups are doing in your town or city and what your council's environmental policy is. If you think it's a bit tame, tell them so!

A Business: The Body Shop International PLC

> "I think you can trade ethically; be committed to social responsibility, global responsibility; empower your employees without being afraid of them. I think you can re-write the book on the way a business can be run."

By her own admission, Anita Roddick is "mouthy and quotable." She has certainly become a household name in the '90s along with The Body Shop which she founded in Brighton in 1976. From one shop the company now has a chain of more than 500 cosmetics and skin care outlets in 38 countries and a gross turnover of £84.5 million. Of course, The Body Shop is out there to make money and so one should not get too dewy-eyed, but there is something very different about it. Behind the rhetoric and the Roddick quotations, it is no exaggeration to say that the book on running a business has been re-written.

Several friends of mine are employees of The Body Shop working either in local shops or at the headquarters in Littlehampton. Because workers are treated with dignity, have opportunities to participate in the business and are encouraged to volunteer for community and other projects, industrial relations are good and morale is high. There is a real commitment not merely to the environment in general but to being an example – printing all its literature and stationery on recycled paper, recycling office aluminium, glass and waste paper and recycling its own post-consumer plastic waste.

The secret behind their success is the management's belief that they must remain a human enterprise linking people – employees, customers, suppliers, franchisees – and must not become a profit-making machine. Espousing values such as integrity, knowledge, humour, candour, creativity, education and respect has certainly confused some people, and drawn cynicism and contempt from parts of the business community. There is no doubt that The Body Shop is usually loved or hated – it is a genuine catalyst, an *agent provocateur*.

I know where I stand – the Roddicks get my vote. They have taken on so many negative assumptions and turned them upside down. Through a commitment to the environment, to fair trade and to human dignity I am sure that Jesus would have described Anita as "close to the Kingdom." Their campaigning: Trade Not Aid; Against Animal Testing; Stop the Burning and Free John McCarthy have constantly challenged the status quo.

Surely this is an example for Christian business people to follow. Once it has been proved it can be done, I hope that more and more people will do it.

A Church

The fact that I have not named a church does not mean that there is not one which is modelling something positive – it's just that I do not know where it is at present!

Such a church would not be "environment crazy", like Greenpeace with a cross in there somewhere. It would be marrying all the distinctive values of the Kingdom of God and expressing them in its worship life, its outreach and its involvement in the community. Sadly, many of the churches which I have seen taking on some form of green agenda appear to have very few other biblical distinctives left!

A Home: 21 Crescent Road, Bognor Regis

I humbly offer our home as a model! It is a model of strengths and weaknesses, successes and failures – certainly not yet an eco-ideal home.

Perhaps we have done best in energy-saving so far (maybe because that saves money as well!) Our house is a turn of the century inner terrace so there are only two outside walls and they are pretty thick. The roof is double-insulated, once between the first floor and the loft, and also between the thermo-board and the slates themselves. Most of the radiators have thermostats and we have a room 'stat and a timer as well. Most of the windows and doors have been draught-insulated, a cheap and cost-effective method of cutting down on heat loss. I recently turned down the thermostat on the water heater by 2° and we didn't notice the loss of heat.

We also have our boiler serviced every year by a man named Kevin which avoids any wasted gas and possible explosions. Wherever possible we have shelled out for low-wattage lightbulbs (the initial outlay is a bit frightening but they last 8–12 times longer than pearl lamps and use a fraction of the electricity). Charlotte is very clever about filling up the oven by cooking two meals at once; using the pressure cooker and this sort of thing. We usually have showers rather than baths (using 29 rather than 90 litres of water) but when we do fill the bath between two and four of us will use the same water – occasionally at the same time!

On the re-use and re-cycling front, we probably score about 6/10. When we go out shopping we take some carrier bags from a previous expedition. If we don't take enough then the extra are used as bin-liners or nappy bags. Our back garden currently has a wide selection of glass awaiting a trip to the bottle-bank, but we don't recycle our paper as there are no facilities for this in the area. (This obviously offers an opportunity for a project soon!) However, I could redeem some points if I had a newspaper-"log" maker, but I don't.

On the down-side, our food supplies could be a bit greener. Charlotte faithfully grows a few organic vegetables in the garden, although there is only so much one can do with a plot 2′ square. We have not yet found a local supplier of organic vegetables or free-range and organic meat, although we usually only eat meat once or twice a week and always buy free-range eggs. Our cleaning products are free of phosphates, bleach and all other materials that would clean anything.

My energy failings include instinctively turning on the central heating if I'm cold rather than putting on a jumper. As for my wife, there's no way I can persuade her to shut the internal doors and neither of us are brilliant at turning off lights.

Whilst writing this, a friend commented that this list looks less like "how to be green" than "how to be *mean*"! The fact that saving resources also often saves money only highlights the fact that a quiet premium has been placed on convenience and the luxury of being able to waste. We must reject those values.

An Individual: You!

The time has come for you to decide where to begin. Do you want to be a positive role model, an example of someone who is seeking to live a whole and wholistic life?

One of the themes which has recurred throughout this book has been that of relationship. I have found that discussing things with family, friends and colleagues has made the process of change more exciting and much easier. Given what I have said about interconnectedness that should not be surprising!

First I recommend that you consider some of the changes you have made over the past months or years to live greener. Hopefully, this will encourage you and give you confidence. Then, why not write down in a few words why you think it is important for you to be more environmentally active. Next make a list of what you consider are the most serious environmental issues and which ones you think you can help reduce. Set a few goals that are measurable and achievable.

The issues can be whatever you like (or whatever God speaks to you about). The kind of environment-conscious choices in the home that I described above are but one dimension to consider – community involvement, reconciliation, free-range food or vegetarianism might all be things that you need to think about.

Conclusion

Whether or not you are reading this as a Christian believer, you have been made in the image of God. Perhaps the greatest evil that any of us could do at this time would be to do nothing. In this generation we have the power to make the greatest impact on our planet. Science and technology have put in our hands the means to alleviate suffering and adminstrate justice on a global scale. Yet still we watch our TV screens and hopelessly witness another "natural disaster", another "act of God". It does not look like the power of technology is going to be used in this way. Rather, the planet will continue to be plundered, the cycles of life disrupted and the health of future generations jeopardised. We should be concerned about the future. After all, we will spend the rest of our lives there.

But this book cannot close on a gloomy or an apocalyptic note. Its theme has been the gospel, the good news of Jesus. He is our hope and the anchor of our souls, "firm and secure".[18] We are securely anchored to an age where there will be a globe, but no global warming; where there will be an ozone layer, but one without any holes in; where the wolf will lie down with the lamb, where the child will play by the viper's nest without fear, and where God himself will wipe away every tear.[19] As citizens of heaven,[20] we are literally looking forward to heaven on earth. This is not a green utopia, but God's own promise.

Best of all this gospel puts us back in touch with God now. We see that we are anchored firmly in the age to come, but live in the present today. Our response must be to live lives of worhsip in word, song and deed. As the hymn-writer wrote:

Were the whole realm of nature mine,
That were a present far too small
Love so amazing, so divine
Demands my soul, my life, my all.

Notes

1 Genesis 3:9.
2 Matthew 16:15.
3 Matthew 22:18 (NASB).
4 Judges 21:25 (NASB).
5 Romans 14:1b.
7 James 1:5.
8 2 Corinthians 5:17.
9 Galatians 3:1; 5:12.
10 Matthew 5:13.
11 Ephesians 6:12.
12 Noel Richards, "Believing the Best" *Danger Line* Word 1987.
13 References throughout are to Richard Kennaway's paper published in *The Round Table* The Commonwealth Journal of International Affairs, January 1991.
14 *CEPAD Report* (News and Analysis for the Evangelical Church in Nicaragua), November 1991.
15 Their address is The Green, Witham Park, Waterside South, Lincoln LN5 7JR.
16 Details for Leicester are available from Ian Roberts, Director of Leicester Environment City, Parkfield, Western Park, Hinckley Road, Leicester LE3 6HX.
18 Hebrews 6:19.
19 Revelation 21:4.
20 See Philippians 3:20.

PART FOUR
APPENDICES

Appendix One

CRACKING THE JARGON

A Glossary of Terms

I hope I don't insult anyone's intelligence with what follows, but it is important that we know what we're talking about! As a layman myself, I have tried to give explanations to and definitions of some words and phrases which once puzzled me. I have also made brief comments on one or two issues which are commonly discussed in the "green debate" but which are not included in the main text of the book.

In order to try to make the subjects as understandable as possible, some of the concepts have been greatly simplified and generalised. This means neither that I think they are simple nor that everyone will agree with the conclusions which I suggest. Further, the word for which you wanted a brief description is just bound to be missing – space simply does not allow for an exhaustive list. However, in both cases, there are many excellent books and magazines which can help you to get into the scientific (or the theological) debates if you wish. Turn excitedly to Appendix 2 for more details of these.

The list is in alphabetical order. The symbol * means that there is a separate entry for the preceding word or phrase.

Acid Rain
Like the greenhouse effect,* acid rain is as natural as the earth itself. Sulphur, one of life's vital minerals, has a highly acidic quality. Most of the sulphur released into the atmosphere comes from bacteria and plants in estuaries and mangrove swamps as sulphur dioxide (SO_2) and hydrogen sulphide. As a highly soluble gas, SO_2 easily gets drawn into the water cycle, and so returns to the ground with rain, mist, snow, and so on.

Coal and other fossil fuels* contain sulphur, and as they are burned the acidity of the rain increases. To separate this from "natural" acid rain, some scientists describe the industrial variety as "super-acid rain". In any case, the increased acidity seeping into the soil causes great damage to the trees downwind of the sulphur-puffing chimneys. It also allows poisonous minerals like aluminium, lead and zinc to flood out into lakes and rivers killing the plant and fish life.

Air Pollution

The air around us can become polluted as a result of our own activities. For instance, when coal is burnt gases and smoke are produced. These can make the air we breathe dirty and unpleasant – sometimes it becomes poisonous.

In 1952 4,000 people died in London as a result of air pollution.[1] This pollution came from coal fires in people's homes, from factories and from power stations. It combined with the winter fog to form a poisonous mixture of smoke and fog, known as *smog*. After this disaster smokeless zones were created by the Clean Air Act of 1956. Undoubtedly urban smoke was reduced, but London air can still hardly be called clean!

Apart from the effects of sulphur dioxide (see Acid Rain*), motor vehicle exhausts are one of the major causes of air pollution today, releasing carbon monoxide and oxides of nitrogen. A difficulty with air pollution is that whilst some forms can be seen, like smoke, the most dangerous gases cannot.

Animism

Animistic beliefs are a primitive faith that a multitude of spirits live in animals, plants, mountains, etcetera. It has been claimed that the spread of the Christian faith has contributed to the crushing of animistic reverence for nature in some tribal situations. When these beliefs are eroded, the argument continues, it becomes easier to convince native peoples to allow the exploitation of the natural resources – forests, rivers and wild animals – which they once worshipped.

It may be true that some gross errors have been made in the name of Christian mission over the course of Church history. The murderous Spanish conquistadors in America and the cultural imperialism of the British in Africa are two examples. However, the question of how beneficial these animistic religions were to their followers, with their rule of superstition and fear, is rarely posed.

In the melting pot of spiritual ideas found in the New Age movement, animistic religions like Shamanism find especial favour, offering an opportunity to "find oneness with God" in nature. In the light of this, Christian environmentalists need to be very careful when we talk about the presence of God within the creation.

Anthropocentric

Make sure you've got your teeth in before attempting to say this one! It simply means "human-centred", and is seen as the original sin by most Greens in general and by those who would hold Gaia* or New Age* views in particular. A Christian worldview will not be anthropocentric (although it is often caricatured as so being), but neither will it be *biocentric* (or biosphere*-centred) as would a "deep Green" worldview. Rather, the biblical view of reality is firmly *theocentric* or God-centred.

As I mentioned in Chapter 6, the despotic attitude to nature which the Greens properly deplore finds its roots neither in the Bible nor in Christian history, but rather in the "rationalist"* tradition. This tradition is founded in the ancient paganism of later Greek thought as revived by modern humanism. To be philosophically accurate, this is known as "the Stoic-Cartesian anthropocentric view of nature."[2] Impress your friends with that one!

Atonement
The theological word which describes the primary work of Jesus on the Cross. Atonement has restored humanity to its rightful dependent relationship with God. Whilst there have been different ways of explaining this idea, it is based upon the fact that Jesus as God's *Son*, came to earth and *suffered*, offering himself as a sacrifice for our *sin*.

Focussing on the theme of this book, I should go on to say that the restoration of humanity to God must lead to the restoration of the whole creation, and to reconciliation within it. Classically, this would not be seen as part of atonement *per se*.

Biodegradable
Substances capable of of being broken down by bacteria and fungi in the soil, or by other environmental processes. "Biodegradable" has become quite a buzz word because of the concern about plastics, metals and other substances in waste which are likely to remain on earth as waste for many hundreds of years to come.

Each household in Britain throws away about a tonne of rubbish every year.[3] If we believe that because a substance is labelled "biodegradable" (or "photodegradable"*) we can trash it without a second thought, there are two major problems. First, the rotting and degrading process gives off methane, a combination of carbon and hydrogen (CH_4). This gas is an excellent fuel, but is only occasionally piped away for use. More usually, it is allowed to escape into the atmosphere (which is bad news as it is a greenhouse gas*) and it can cause serious explosions.

Second, because landfill* sites are often heavily compressed down, it is unlikely that any bacteria ever get to do their biodegrading deeper than a few feet below the surface. For example, some bright spark recently decided to drill down into a New York landfill. All the 1960's newspapers he found were still easily readable!

Biosphere
The earth and its atmosphere – all our planet's living things and the physical environment in which they exist. The phrase "global ecosystem" is often used to describe the interconnected nature of all life. In this book I have sometimes used the term earth* interchangeably with biosphere.

Carbon Dioxide (CO_2)
This gas is one of the natural ingredients of air and is a vital part of the carbon cycle. It is produced when animals breathe out and when any material containing carbon is burned. Plants use $C0_2$ as a food, mixing it with water and sunlight to produce sugars. This process is known as photosynthesis and is the source of food for almost all living organisms. CO_2 is not a toxin,* but it cannot support life alone and therefore can suffocate.

The build-up of CO_2 in the atmosphere currently threatens to upset the balance of gases and so cause global-warming.* The main causes of this build-up are emissions from the burning of fossil fuels* and the destruction of the earth's tropical rainforests.

Chlorofluorocarbons (CFCs)
Chlorine-based compounds used as aerosol propellants, refrigerants, coolants, sterilants, solvents and in the production of insulating foam packaging used by the fast food industry. CFCs take a long time to break down (up to 100 years) and therefore atmospheric levels have risen sharply as industry has found more and uses for these gases.

CFCs have become an ecological demon because they are connected with two problems of air pollution. First, they are greenhouse gases* and therefore are thought to contribute to global-warming.* Second, they are seen to be responsible for the depletion of the stratospheric ozone layer – first made famous by the discovery of an "ozone hole" over Antarctica. The US Environmental Protection Agency project that ozone loss will cause 200,000 additional skin-cancer deaths in the US alone over the next 50 years.[4]

Most nations are planning to cut or ban the use of CFCs by the end of the century. Unfortunately, nearly all the newer propellants and other replacements for CFCs are still greenhouse gases.* Therefore, aerosols should still be avoided.

Conservation
As the word implies, this is about conserving species and habitats from destruction. Described as applying the principles of ecology, it includes treating natural resources in a manner which prevents their unnecessary waste or damage. Thus the ecological balance of the varieties of living species and their habitats is sustained, and their survival ensured. (See Chapter 8 for comments on conservation).

Covenant
A common form of contractual agreement between two partners in the ancient world.

In the Bible, when God made a covenant, it was more one-sided, reflecting his unconditional faithfulness. However, in terms of fulfilment, covenants were mutual, or two-sided – his people were commanded to keep the covenant through love and obedience. The most important examples include the Lord's covenants with Noah (Genesis 6:18 and 9:1–17), with Abraham (Genesis 15) and with Moses (Exodus 6:4ff). In at least two of these, animals come within the scope of God's promises.

Deforestation

> "Twenty-two years ago, forests covered one-quarter of the world's land surface. They now cover one-fifth".[5]

The stripping of one of the globe's vital resources – trees. They clean the air, conserve the soil, maintain its fertility, store water, provide a habitat for wildlife and play a critical role in regulating climate. The loss of forests – and tropical rainforests* in particular – are rightly one of the greatest ecological concerns of this generation.

Globally, 12.5 million hectares of forest are being lost every year – an area the size of the state of Mississippi or Austria and Switzerland combined.[6] The Amazonian forests, the world's largest, have shrunk from their original size of around 4.8 million km^2 to 3.8 million km^2.[7] The reasons for deforestation are many and varied: population pressures, debt servicing, accelerated growth policies and many others. As far as the Amazon is concerned, its development has been described as a gigantic game of Monopoly, with federal governments, the World Bank and the USA as the chief players.[8] As ever, it is only too easy to guess who will be the losers: the indigenous Amerindian tribes, the poor settlers and the life of the forests themselves.

Deism
Whilst this movement has been described as "a spent force and a non-combatant in 20th-century theological battles",[9] some of its supporters could be described as the "Pre-Greens" of the 18th and 19th centuries.[10] Further, many people today who view established Christianity at its most dead and boring, appear to hold a view similar to deism.

Deism is popularly pictured as stating that God is a kind, but remote creator. This idea is a product of the age of reason, and is often illustrated by showing the world as a huge and complex clock. This clock has been made and wound up by God, who does not have anything further to do with it. The clock now seems to be winding down to its destruction.

The odd miracle or two would obviously be a tough challenge to the Deist!

Desertification
This is not a mechanised way of producing puddings and sweets, but a big word for the spread of deserts. There are numerous reasons for desertification, including poor agricultural methods and land management, deforestation* and air pollution* which can cause damage to forests.

Desertification is closely linked with soil erosion.*

Dualism
See Gnosticism* and Chapter 6.

Earth
The dictionary tells us that the earth is the third planet in order from the sun, but I'm sure that most readers will know how to find it! In this book the "earth" is used to mean the whole planet – dry land, sea, freshwater and atmosphere. The scientific word for this definition is biosphere*.

Ecological Crisis
This is a very broad term which describes the crisis in our ecology* (surprise, surprise!). The intricate relationship between man, plants, animals and the earth is in a mess – it's "out of synch.". It is not just a series of different problems; each has an effect on another.

For example, too many cars cause too much carbon* emission, too many toxins* in the atmosphere and need too many new roads. The knock-on effects are that carbon emissions increase global warming*; toxins contribute to acid rain*; and road-building threatens agricultural land and natural habitats. Among other things, global warming causes sea-levels to rise; acid rain kills rivers, lakes and forests; loss of agricultural land can encourage intensive farming methods and loss of natural habitat can endanger species. And so it goes on. Think about that next time you jump in your car to buy a pint of milk!

Chapter 3 describes how we have caused havoc with the delicate balances and cycles which God has built into this planet. If there is a particular issue that concerns you, whether it be saving the whales or campaigning for the rainforests, remember that everything is linked. Don't get locked into one issue; let's tackle the whole crisis. Global problems need wholistic solutions.

Ecology
If it ends in 'ology' it's bound to be complicated! In a nutshell, we are talking about the study of life in relation to its environment. The Greek root is *oikos* which means 'house'. Therefore the idea is to look at the plants, animals and people as part of the big picture of where they live – that is, the earth.* For this reason, we can say that "ecological" is broader than "environmental": the environment concerns our surroundings whereas ecology is about how everything fits together.

Ecosystems
Self-sufficient units of systems in nature with simple or complex cycles, involving both living organisms and non-living matter.

Environment
Our surroundings – the natural and social conditions which constitute the quality of life. Environmentalism is about taking an interest in those surroundings.

Erosion
The removal of topsoil due to the action of wind and rain. Under natural conditions, erosion would take place slowly and the lost soil would be replaced by decaying organic* matter. However, deforestation*, overgrazing and poor agricultural practices have contributed to an alarming increase in the rate of soil loss today. In the most vulnerable agricultural areas, soil erosion leads directly to desertification and thereby land is lost to all production.

Some examples of this trend include Australia, where one tonne of topsoil is lost for every six tonnes of produce grown; Ethiopia, where annual topsoil losses amount to some 1,600 million tonnes; India where some 300,000 square miles of land are affected and the

USA where one-third of all crop-land is seriously affected by erosion.[11]

Fossil Fuels
Fossils are made of the traces of living things which have been preserved in rocks. Fossilisation occurs when living things die and are buried under great pressure which prevents them decaying. They can then undergo different physical changes depending on various factors.

"Fossil fuels" describe coal, gas and oil which were produced by fossilisation and preserve the carbon which was present in the previous (usually vegetable) life-form. Fossil fuels are burned, or "combusted", for transportation, the generation of electricity and industrial, commercial and domestic energy use. This combustion releases about 6,000,000,000 (that is, a lot) of carbon into the atmosphere as carbon dioxide.*[12]

Gaia
Originated by a scientist named James Lovelock in the 1970s, the "Gaia Hypothesis" is the sort of strange mix of science and Eastern spirituality which has become a distinctive feature of the New Age movement.* It proposes that the earth is a single organism and that all life on earth represent no more than different parts of the whole.

The name "Gaia" is that of the pagan Greek earth goddess. This hypothesis has gained great popularity beyond the bounds of New Age writers, but is very firmly based in monism* and pantheism.*

Global
Something which is world-wide or affects the whole earth.

Global-warming
The effect on the world's climate of the enhanced impact of the greenhouse-effect.* A 'hot' scientific debate rages as to whether the climate is changing at all, and if so whether or not the changes are due to human activity. During the 1970s it was recognised that increased levels of carbon dioxide (CO_2)* could potentially enhance the greenhouse-effect. Nobody then believed it had affected the climate – indeed some scientists thought that it was equally possible that air pollution* might block out so much radiation from the sun that the earth's climate would get colder!

Since then further facts have become clear. At least five of the hottest global* years of the century occurred in the 1980s[13] and a rise in sea levels has already been detected in some areas. The evidence is by no means undisputed and one of the most recent reports, by the Meteorological Office, suggests that average temperatures will rise by no more than 1.5°C over the next 70 years – only a fraction of the "doomsday predictions" made by some environmentalists.[14] On the other hand, a panel of several hundred scientists have stated a belief that while changes in the climate might be slow at present, calamitous changes could follow at a rate to which it would be impossible to adjust.[15]

However, most people agree that if we wait for concrete evidence before attempting to reduce the impact of the greenhouse-effect, it will probably be too late.

Gnosticism

One of the oldest perversions of Christian doctrine, thought to have been around as early as the first century. It is basically a mixture of orthodox Christianity and certain Greek philosophical ideas, emphasising a dualism – an opposition between the spiritual world and the evil, material world.

The gnostic way of salvation is through knowledge (*gnosis* in Greek) received through special revelation from God. The basic flaw of the gnostics is that they create a kind of two-tier Christianity, separating those who have and those who have not received secret knowledge. It means that salvation is no longer through Christ alone.

What is the significance of all this from an ecological perspective? First, the brand of dualism found in some churches today and described in Chapter 6, bears similarities to gnosticism in its low view of the material world. Second, many of the strands of this thinking fuelled the secular rationalism* of the Age of Enlightenment: the period of new ideas which opened the way to scientific dominance over nature.

Greenhouse effect

This now very familiar phrase presents the picture of the earth* as a global* greenhouse. In an ordinary greenhouse it is the glass which lets the sunlight in, but prevents the heat from escaping. In our atmosphere it is the "greenhouse gases"* which act like the glass in a gardener's greenhouse.

Many gases in the atmosphere allow sunlight to pass through but soak up some of the infra-red radiation given off by the earth's heated surface. The natural amounts of these greenhouse gases present in the earth raise the average temperature of the air above the surface by about 35°C. Without these gases life on earth would be virtually impossible – the average surface temperature would not rise above a rather chilly –20°C.[16]

There is no argument that the greenhouse effect exists. But the phrase is often used to describe how human activity, particularly the burning of fossil fuels*, has caused enhanced global warming.* This is looked at more closely in chapter 3.

Greenhouse Gases
The chief greenhouse gases are water vapour, carbon dioxide,* methane and nitrous oxide, all of which occur naturally. In addition, there are man-made chemicals, especially CFCs* which contribute to the greenhouse effect.*

Greenness
Broadly defined as an awareness of ecological principles, this familiar phrase is highly imprecise. It will involve responding to life as a whole with particular sensitivity to the needs of long-term inter-relationships between people and the planet. However, as mentioned in Chapter 7, greenness must bring all other issues within its scope. If "green" is no more than an isolated issue or idea separate from the rest of reality, it has failed in its very reason for existence.

Groundwater
Water held in underground rocks and soil. It comes mainly from water seeping down from the surface.

Hamburgers
There is a lot of talk about eating hamburgers being bad for the environment. What is it all about?

In a nutshell, the main problems at present are focussed in Central and South America. Demand for cheap hamburger meat has led to the clearing of huge forests there for cattle ranching. Someone has worked out that a staggering 9 SQUARE MILES OF FOREST ARE CLEARED FOR EACH HAMBURGER![18] The burning of the forest and, unlikely as it may sound, natural digestive fermentation in cattle (that is, belching) together produce 39% of the methane rising from the tropics. Methane is a greenhouse gas.*

The ecological destruction caused by ranching programmes is long-term and often irreversible. Once deprived of tree cover, the land quickly deteriorates and within a few years has to be abandoned. On top of the climatic and other problems of deforestation,* the loss of tree cover to billions of birds is proving catastrophic for American continental migration patterns.

The claim of McDonald's that they do not use beef from Central

America in their US restaurants is impossible to disprove. Once it enters the US domestic market it becomes indistinguishable from home-raised beef.

Insecticides
Chemicals used to kill harmful or irritating insects, though often used against other animal pests as well. Unfortunately, the increased use of insecticides and other pesticides over the past forty years has created some major environmental problems. The poisons they contain are rarely selective and can travel up the food chain. This has led to damage caused to such species as otters, birds of prey and seals in Europe. There have also been cases of human poisoning.

Landfill
A common method of waste disposal, used to deal with most of the world's hazardous and domestic wastes. Methods vary from the primitive tipping of left-overs into a hole in the ground, to more "sanitary" techniques.[19]

Throughout the industrialised world, concern has been expressed about the seepage of dangerous substances into rivers, seas and groundwater* supplies. In the UK, the official watchdog agency, HWI (Hazardous Waste Inspectorate) has severely criticised the management of British landfills. It is estimated that 1,390 landfills are in danger of explosion – 756 within metres of housing.[20]

Monism
All reality is ultimately one. God is therefore one expression of the all-inclusive Absolute Being, rather than being the one eternal reality.

Monism denies the God-creation distinction which is so essential to all theistic* religions, including Christianity. This is what leads to pantheism* and other similar world-views popular with the New Age movement.*

New Age Movement
See Chapter 8.

Organic Farming
Farming without the aid of artificial fertilisers, synthetic insecticides, growth hormones and other ecologically-harmful "agrochemicals". Whilst "organic" more precisely describes chemical-free farming, its use has been expanded to embrace other practices which are less destructive and violent to land and animals: free-range poultry farming,

humane slaughtering conditions, crop rotation, no straw-burning or hedge-grubbing.

Although in the late 1980s organic food was still around 35% more expensive than non-organic,[21] the market is now moving slowly to show that this is changing. The more of us buying organic, the quicker the change! In addition, when it comes to meat production, some dreadful farming practices have clearly been a factor in the recent incidents of salmonella, BSE and other diseases. In spite of government health assurances, it seems that we are reaping a bitter harvest for our greedy intensive production.

Ozone layer
See Chlorofluorocarbons.*

Panentheism
The view that the universe is God, although God is more than the universe. It is clearly distinct from pantheism* where God and the universe are completely identical.

One of the best known illustrations of the panentheist view of God is to compare God's relation to the universe with a person's relation to their body. I depend on my body as the source of my experience, but I am more than my body. Thus, "while God depends on his body, the universe, he also transcends it, as a mind that knows all of the possibilities for future events."[22]

This view challenges traditional beliefs about the omnipotence of God, and about his place completely outside of time and space. However, it does go some of the way to explaining the mysterious relationship between God and his creation.

Pantheism
A spiritual view of the world derived from the Greek *pan* (all) and *theos* (God). This gives a fair idea of the meaning: "all is God". The two basic principles of pantheism are that everything is one and that this unity is divine.

It agrees with biblical Christianity and other theistic ideas in affirming that the world depends upon God. However, the drastic difference from theism* is that pantheism does not accept that the world's existence is separate to the existence of God.

Photodegradable
Substances capable of of being broken down by light – sunlight in particular. The problems with packaging labelled with this word are discussed under Biodegradable.*

Photosynthesis
See Carbon Dioxide*

Population
The world population currently stands at around 6 billion – five times the level at which it stood in 1800. Today, 150 babies are being born every minute somewhere on earth, and ninety per cent of growth predicted over the next century will occur in the Third World.[23]

Under present economic conditions, the planet simply cannot sustain this growth. Deforestation,* soil erosion* and desertification* are all direct results of population pressures. The increasing standard of living of industrialised societies, the growing of cash crops for export, and the "paving over" of so much agricultural land are all factors which make feeding more and more people harder. For example, a single Western child will use about forty times more of the world's resources than a child born in the Third World![24]

In the light of this, it can be seen that family planning is only a very small part of the solution.

Rationalism
The "Age of Reason" is generally described as that period of history in Europe between the Peace of Westphalia (1648) and the French Revolution (1789) when "the issues which occupied men's minds and the spirit in which they were debated carry us from an atmosphere still predominantly medieval to one which is essentially modern."[25] It was during this period that men like Locke, Descartes and Voltaire fearlessly challenged the view of the world presented by the Church, and replaced it by one which was subject to "reason". Drawing on later Greek thought, the modern age – and with it the modern religion of secular humanism – was born.

As far as the Creation is concerned, rationalism paved the way for man's conquest of nature through science and technology. It is this humanistic emphasis, rather than the Church's teaching in recent centuries, that truly lies at the heart of so much of the present ecological crisis.

Recycling
The idea of using materials again in a different form. Things like milk-bottles and paper which has been used on one side only can be re-used. This is the best way of saving energy and resources. If an item cannot be used any more in its present form, the substances which construct it can be re-cycled into another item. This is an important way of cutting down on waste and saving resources.

For example, in the United Kingdom 6,000 million bottles and jars are thrown away each year. 2 million tonnes of glass ends up in landfill sites – never to be used again and certainly non-biodegradable. However it is estimated that 6 million people are using bottle banks each week, and in 1987 750 million bottles and jars were recycled.[26]

It has rightly been observed that the earth is the ultimate recyclist, using the same basic elements and compounds of water, oxygen, carbon, phosphorus, nitrogen and sulphur over and over again. All this is powered by the energy of the sun, enabling life to continue and all things to be sustained.

Sulphur
See acid rain*

Sustainability
A real green buzz-word is this, and a very important concept as well. It has been defined as "the ability to indefinitely maintain a way of life without excessive damage to the Planet and to future generations."[27] The parallel idea of "sustainable development" is that which "meets the needs of the present without compromising the ability of future generations to meet their own needs."[28] Thus, a sustainable lifestyle is one which treads lightly on the earth's resources. The ultimate aim is to handle the earth in a manner which ensures the continuance of life systems in all their variety.

Sustainability is all about doing minimum damage, creating minimum waste and *meeting need*, rather than *satisfying greed*. It could be argued that Jesus' command that we pray, "give us this day our daily bread",[29] speaks of a moderate, simple and sustainable model of lifestyle. Of course, no reader of the gospels could ignore the fact that this is the way that Jesus himself lived.

Theism
In a broad sense, belief in God. It is usually used to distinguish the religions of Christianity, Islam and Judaism – which all believe in a personal creator-God, who is self-revealing, active in creation and therefore worthy of worship – from other spiritual world-views. In particular, it contrasts with two other "isms". One is pantheism*, which does not acknowledge a personal creator-God who is separate from the world. The other is deism*, which does not accept that God is still active in the world.

Tobacco
No one needs to be told about the health implications of smoking

– the ecological effects are much less well known. Producing tobacco ruins the soil and because it is often grown in semi-arid areas this degradation often leads to desertification.* Worse still is the destruction caused to forests to create fuel for tobacco-curing barns. Trees from an estimated 4,600 square miles are cut down each year for this purpose.[30]

For many Third World countries, tobacco is an important cash crop, but it takes up 0.3% of the world's available arable land.[31] This land could be used to produce food for domestic consumption or for export.

Toxins
Poisons of organic origin.

Tropical Rainforests
Running around the equator, the tropical forests occupy some three and a half million square miles and one quarter of the world's people depend on them for water.[32] These are but two of the staggering statistics which explain why the wholesale destruction of such vast areas of forest is creating such an ecological panic.

Although rainforests are still to be found in Central Africa and tropical Asia, the bulk of the remainder are located in Amazonia, and most of Amazonia lies in Brazil.[33] The forests generally grow on very poor soil, with complex and highly efficient in-built sytems which recycle minerals. Indeed, the apocryphal remark that the Amazon is a desert covered by trees is not far wrong.[34] In almost all cases where forests are cleared, the soil is soon eroded away rendering the land sterile within a few years.

Apart from the incredible volume and variety of species which they contain,[35] rainforests are globally important because they absorb carbon dioxide ($C0_2$)* and through a process known as evapotranspiration reduce extremes of temperature both in the tropics and in temperate zones (see climate zones*). The burning of forests is thus a double-edged sword: reducing the number of trees able to absorb $C0_2$ and releasing huge amounts of carbon into the atmosphere as smoke. The overall result is most likely to be an enhancing of the greenhouse effect.*

Deforestation* is one of the greatest of all ecological problems. Daring plans are needed to secure the future of forests. Some environmentalists have suggested that governments could exchange their forests for their debts to Northern banks (see Chapter 9). The land would be held by an international body as a world park. A small step in this direction has already been taken in Bolivia. On the negative side, the Brazilian government asked that the seven major industrialised nations contribute $1.6 billion in financial assistance to help preserve the rainforest. So far, only $50 million has been committed. As Ian McCluskey notes, "Money, pride and politics seem to roil the debate about conservation; and as the arguments heat up, so do the flames in the rain forest."[36]

Notes

1 Friends of the Earth
2 Richard Russell *Conservation and Creation* Biblical Creation, numbers 15 and 16.
3 Baines and James *The Cycles of Life* BBC Education, 1991, p 20.
4 *Time* November 1991, p 54.
5 Global 2000 Report to President Carter, 1978.
6 CEPAD Report, November 1991.
7 N Myers *Deforestation Rates in Tropical Forests and their Climatic Implications* London, Friends of the Earth, 1989, pp 13–26.
8 A Gross *Amazonia in the Nineties: sustainable development or another decade of destruction?* Third World Quarterly 12(3), July 1990, p 6.
9 S N Williams *Deism* in "Dictionary of Theology", IVP 1988, p 190
10 Eg Thomas Paine (1737–1809).
11 Goldsmith and Hildyard *The Earth Report 2* Mitchell Beazley 1990, p 65.
12 Shell Briefing Service, Number 5, 1990, p 2.
13 According to Nasa scientist, James Hansen as quoted in *The Guardian* 5 July 1988.
14 Reported in *The Sunday Times* 29 December 1991.
15 Report of the UN's Intergovernmental Panel on Climate Change, reported in *The Guardian* 13 February 1992.
16 Shell Briefing Service *ibid.*, p 1.
17 *Earth Report 2*, *ibid.*, p 89.
18 *Ibid.*, p 100.
19 *Ibid.*
20 Elkington, Burke and Hailes *Green Pages* Routledge 1988, p 144.
21 W D Beck *Panentheism in* "Dictionary of Theology", p 487.
22 *Earth Report 2*, *ibid.*, p 130.
23 *Ibid.*
24 Gerald R Cragg *The Church and the Age of Reason* Penguin 1960, p 13.
25 Wright and Baines *ibid.*, p 7.
26 Christian Ecology Link resource pack, *Christians and the Planet* CEL 1990.
27 World Commission on Environment and Development, p 43.
28 Luke 11:3.
29 *Earth Report 2*, *ibid.*, p 155.

30 *Ibid.*
31 *Ibid.*, p 159.
32 The total extent of moist forests in the world is now about 8 million square kilometres. Of this, Brazil holds 2.2 million square kilometres. N Myers *Ibid.*
33 A Gross *Ibid.*, p 7.
34 For example, the Amazon contains one in five of every bird species and at least two thousand species of fish. There are perhaps thirty million animal species in all, most of which are insects. *Ibid.*
35 *Time* 28 October 1991, pp 42,43.

Appendix Two

SOME USEFUL HOT-TIPS

Books and Addresses

You will find here a brief bibliography arranged by topics, offering further reading on subjects which I have touched upon in this book. I have then provided some addresses and telephone numbers of organisations and groups which may be of help or interest if you wish to take things further. I do not necessarily subscribe to all the views represented.

1. BIBLIOGRAPHY

The following list of books under a variety of topics are a mix of doctrinal, teaching, factual and practical titles. Most are written from a Christian point of view, but some are not.

Theological books have a notorious reputation as being a cure for insomnia and incomprehensible to boot. There are a few notable exceptions to this caricature but they nearly all require quite a bit of brain-work!

Animals

K Barth, *Church Dogmatics, Vol.3* Edinburgh 1936–81
A Linzey, *Animal Rights,* London 1976
The Status of Animals in the Christian Tradition, Birmingham 1985
Christianity and the Rights of Animals, London 1987
D L Williams, *Assault and Battery*, "Third Way" 9:7 1987
Animal Rights in New Dictionary of Theology (NDT), Leicester 1988
R Griffiths, *The Human Use of Animals*, Bramcote 1979

Apologetics

S Gaukroger, *It Makes Sense*
J McDowell, *Evidence That Demands a Verdict*
J McDowell, *More Than a Carpenter*

Biblical Worldview
S Bishop and C Droop, *The Earth is the Lord's*, Bristol 1990
B Goudzwaard, *Idols of our Time*, Downer's Grove 1984
B J Walsh and J R Middleton, *The Transforming Vision*, Downer's Grove 1984
A Wolters, *Creation Regained*, Leicester 1986
O Guinness, *The Gravedigger File*, Leicester 1983
S Shaw, *No Splits,* London 1989

Creation
O R Barclay, *Creation* in NDT
H Blocher, *In the Beginning*, Leicester 1984
E Brunner, *Dogmatics 2: The Christian Doctrine of Creation and Redemption*, London 1952
D C Burke (ed), *Creation and Evolution*, Leicester 1985
R Forster and P Marston, *Reason and Faith*, Eastbourne 1989
K Heim, *The World: Its Creation and Consummation*, Edinburgh 1962
R Hooykas, *Religion and the Rise of Modern Science*, Edinburgh 1972
K L McKay, *Creation* in New Bible Dictionary (NBD), Leicester 1962
F A Shaeffer, *Genesis in Space and Time*, London 1972
A N Triton, *Whose World?*, London 1970

Environmental Issues (Children)
D Bellamy, *How Green are You?*, 1991
N Butterworth and M Inkpen, *Wonderful Earth!*, Alton 1990
S Seidenberg, *Ecology (My First Library)*, 1990
D Silver and B Valleley, *The Young Person's Guide to Saving the Planet*, 1990
R Spurgeon, *Ecology*, London 1988

Environmental Issues (Adult)
D Bellamy and B Quayle, *Turning the Tide*, 1986
L R Brown, *State of the World 1988*, New York 1988
J Button, *How to be Green*, London 1989
J Elkington, T Burke, J Hailes, *Green Pages*, London 1988
J Elkington and J Hailes, *The Green Consumer Guide*, 1988
E Goldsmith and N Hildyard, *The Earth Report*, London 1988
Green Party, *Manifesto for a Sustainable Society*, London 1990
N Middleton, *Atlas of Environmental Issues*, Oxford 1988
G Lean, D Hinrichsen, A Markham, *Atlas of the Environment*, London 1990
J Porritt, *Seeing Green*, Oxford 1984

Environmental Issues (Christian Perspectives)
T Cooper, *Green Christianity*, London 1990
E Echlin, *The Green Christian Heritage*, (*Grove*) 1989
W Granberg-Michaelson (ed.), *Tending the Garden*, Grand Rapids 1987
K Innes, *Caring for the Earth*, (*Grove*) 1987
S McDonagh, *The Greening of the Church*, London 1990
R Moss, *The Earth in Our Hands*, Leicester 1982
L Osborn, *Steward of Creation*, (*Latimer Hs.*) 1990
C von Ruthland, *Going Green*, London 1991
J R W Stott, *Issues Facing Christians Today*, (Marshalls) 1984

The Fall
K Barth, *Church Dogmatics, Vol.4*, Edinburgh 1936–81
G C Berkouwer, *Sin*, Grand Rapids 1971
J Calvin, *Institutes, Vol.2*
J E Colwell, *Fall* in NBD
M Luther, *The Bondage of the Will*, 1525
D B Milne, *Know the Truth*, Leicester, 1982
J Murray, *The Imputation of Adam's Sin*, Grand Rapids, 1959
H Rondet, *Original Sin*, Shannon, 1971
N P Williams, *The Ideas of the Fall and of Original Sin*, London, 1929

The Kingdom of God
G R Beasley-Murray, *Jesus and the Kingdom of God*, Exeter, 1986
O Cullman, *Salvation In History*, New York, 1967
M Goldsmith, *Kingdom Life*
Oz Guiness, *Gravedigger File*
D Kraybill, *Upside Down Kingdom*
W G Kummel, *Promise and Fulfilment*, London, 1957
G E Ladd, *A Theology of the New Testament*, Grand Rapids, 1974
G E Ladd, *The Gospel of the Kingdom*
G E Ladd, *Living in the Presence of the Future*
R Mitchell, *The Kingdom Factor*, Basingstoke, 1986
H Snyder, *Liberating the Church*
J Wimber, *Power Evangelism*

The New Age movement
R Chandler, *Understanding the New Age*, London 1988
A Clarke and R Ellis, *The New Age and You*, Eastbourne 1991
R Ellis, *The Occult and Young People*, Eastbourne 1989
Loren Wilkinson's essay "New Age, New Consciousness and the New Creation" in *Tending the Garden* (Ed. W. Granberg-Michaelson), Grand Rapids, 1987

Third World and Development Issues
S George, *How the Other Half Dies*, London 1976
S George, *A Fate Worse than Debt*, London 1988
K Keay, *How to Make the World Less Hungry*, Leicester 1990
E F Schumacher, *Small is Beautiful*, London 1974
R J Sider, *Rich Christians in an Age of Hunger*, London 1978
J V Taylor, *Enough is Enough*, London 1975

2. ADDRESSES FOR FURTHER READING AND FOR ACTION

Needless to say, this is only a small selection of the groups and charities who are involved with some form of green activity. I have listed the national addresses and phone numbers (where possible) of the largest and/or best of the organisations. Your library will have details of more localised groups and national headquarters can let you know about their own local groups, eg Friends of the Earth, Green Party, Movement for Christian Democracy.

Alternative Technology and Energy Conservation

Alternate Technology Group
Open University, Milton Keynes, Buckinghamshire.
National Centre For Alternative Technology
Llwyngwern Quarry, Machynlleth, Powys SY20 9AZ
Energy Conservation And Solar Centre
PO Box 1802, London NW1 9RW
Urban Centre for Appropriate Technology
82 Colston Street, Bristol BS1

Animals, Agriculture and Healthy Meat

Animal Christian Concern
46 St Margarets Road, Horsforth, Leeds, West Yorkshire LS18 5BG
British Union for the Abolition of Vivisection
16A Crane Grove, London N7 8LB
Compassion in World Farming
20 Lavant Street, Petersfield, Hampshire GU32 3EW
Free-range Egg Association
37 Tanza Road, London NW3 2UA
Lynx
PO Boz 509, Dunmow, Essex CM6 1UH
Organic Growers Association
Aeron Park, Llangietho, Dyfed
Pure Meat Company
Coombe Court Farm, Moretonhampstead, Devon TQ13 8QD

Real Meat Company
East Hill Farm, Heytesbury, Warminster, Wiltshire BA12 OHR
Royal Society for the Prevention of Cruelty to Animals (RSPCA)
Causeway, Horsham, West Sussex RH12 1HG. Tel: 0403 64181
The Soil Association Ltd.
86 Colston Street, Bristol BS1 5BB
Vegetarian Society
Parkdale, Dunham Road, Altrincham, Cheshire WA14 4QG

Christian Study Materials
Christian Impact
St Peter's Church, Vere Street, London W1
Christian Rural Trust
Manor House Farm, Calton, Waterhouses, Staffs. ST10 3JS
Christian Studies Unit
Widcombe Vicarage, 65 Prior Park Road, Bath BA2 4NL. Tel: 0225 310580
Open Christian College
243 Newbridge Road, Bath BA1 3HJ

General Environmental Groups
Christian Ecology Link
17 Burns Garden, Lincoln, Lincs LN2 4LJ. Tel: 0522 529643
Earthwatch Europe
Belsyre Court, Observatory Road, Oxford OX2 6HU
Friends of the Earth
28-26 Underwood Street, London N1 7JQ. Tel: 071 490 1555
Greenpeace
36 Graham Street, London N1 8LL. Tel: 071 354 5100
Think Green
Premier House, 43/8 New Street, Birmingham B2 4L

Government Bodies
Department of the Environment
Central Unit, Room A302, 43 Marsham Street, London SW7 2AR
Local Government
Telephone your local town hall and ask for the name and address of the department which is responsible for the environment. It will be called something like "Environment and Leisure" or "Environmental Services".

Organic Food and Gardening

Henry Doubleday Research Association
National Centre for Organic Gardening, Ryton-on-Dunsmore, Coventry CV8 3LG

The Soil Association Ltd.
(See under Animals and Agriculture)

Working Weekends on Organic Farms
19 Bradford Road, Lewes, East Sussex BN7 1RB

Political Groups

Christian Socialist Movement
36 Cross Flats Avenue, Leeds LS11 7BG

Conservative Family Campaign
April Cottage, 2 Long Fore, Godalming, Surrey GU7 3TD

Green Party
10 Station Parade, Balham High Road, London SW12 9AZ Tel: 071 738 6721

Liberal Democrats Christian Forum
Heather Hill, Southampton Road, Lyndhurst, Hampshire SO34 7BQ

Movement for Christian Democracy
c/o David Alton MP and Ken Hargreaves MP, House of Commons, London SW1A 0AA. Tel: 071 219 5656

Third World and Fair Trade

CAFOD
2 Romero Close, Stockwell Road, London SW9 9TY. Tel: 071 733 7900

Christian Aid
PO Box 100, London SE1 7RT. Tel: 071 620 4440

Equal Exchange
29 Nicholson Square, Edinburgh EH8 9BX

OXFAM
274 Banbury Road, Oxford OX2 7DZ

TEAR Fund
100 Church road, Teddington, Middlesex

Traidcraft
Kingsway, Gateshead, Tyne and Wear, NE11 0NE. Tel: 091 487 3191

Twin Trading
345 Goswell Road, London EC1V 7JT

Voluntary Service Overseas
9 Belgrave Square, London SW1X 8PW

World Development Movement
Bedford Chambers, Covent Garden, London WC2E 8HA

World Vision
Dychurch House, 8 Abington Street, Northampton NN1 2AJ

Wildlife and Habitat Conservation

British Trust for Conservation Volunteers
36 St Mary's Street, Wallingford, Oxon 0X10 0EU
British Trust for Ornithology
The Nunnery, Nunnery Place, Thetford, Norfolk IP24 2PU. Tel: 0842 750050
Civic Trust
17 Carlton House Terrace, London SW1Y 5AW
Council for the Protection of Rural England
25–27 Buckingham Palace Road, London SW1W OPP. Tel: 071 976 6433
Countryside Commision
John Dower House, Crescent Place, Cheltenham, Glos. GI50 3RA
International Council for Bird Preservation (ICBP)
32 Cambridge Road, Girton, Cambridge CB3 0PJ
London Wildlife Trust
Freepost, London N1 9BR
Marine Conservation Society
9 Gloucester Road, Ross-on-Wye, HR9 5BU
National Trust
36 Queen Anne's Gate, London SW1H 9AS
Royal Society for the Protection of Birds
The Lodge, Sandy, Bedfordshire SG19 2DL. Tel: 0767 80551
Whale and Dolphin Conservation Society
19A James Street West, Bath, Avon BA1 2BT
Watch Trust for Environmental Education
The Green, Witham Park, Lincoln LN5 7JR. Tel: 0522 752326
Wildfowl and Wetland Trust
Slimbridge, Gloucestershire GL2 7BT
Woodland Trust
Autumn Trust, Dysart Road, Grantham, Lincolnshire NG31 6LL
World Wide Fund for Nature
Panda House, Godalming, Surrey. Tel: 0483 426444

Work and Money

Co-operative Development Agency
Broadmead House, 21 Panton Street, London SW1Y 4DR
The Ecology Building Society
8 Main Street, Crosshills, Keighley, West Yorkshire BD20 8TB

The Ethical Investment Research and Information Service
401 Bondway Business Centre, 71 Bondway, London SW8 1SQ
Health and Safety Executive
Baynards House, 1 Chepstow Place, London W2 4TF
Mailing Preference Service
Freepost 22, London W1E 7EZ
New Consumer
52 Elswick Road, Newcastle-upon-Tyne NE4 6JH

3. OTHER RESOURCES

Resources for an Environmental Audit
A highly practical way of assessing whether or not your own home, church premises, school or workplace are responding to the challenge of sustainability, is to do a green audit. Here are some categories with relevant addresses.

Churchyards and premises
Advice on developing churchyards as natural habitats:

Church and Conservation Project
National Agricultural Centre, Stoneleigh, Warwickshire CV8 2LZ
Church of Scotland reports, *Making the most of it* and *Making more of it* on energy-saving measures for church buildings:
Church of Scotland SRT Project
121 George Street, Edinburgh

Energy conservation
A very useful leaflet *The Greenhouse Effect and You* has been produced by WWF (see above for address) and the Consumer's Association.

Ethical investments
Advice can be obtained from:

The Ethical Investment Fund
10 Queen Street, London W1X 7PD. Tel: 081-491-1558
Kingswood Consultants
68 Sheep Street, Bicester, Oxfordshire OX6 7LD. Tel: 0869 252545

Recycled paper
The Association of Recycled Paper Suppliers
Bow Triangle Business Centre, Unit 2, Eleanor Street, London E3 4NP